Drugstore and Soda Fountain Antiques

Douglas Congdon-Martin

Schiffer Publishing Ltd

1469 Morstein Road, West Chester, Pennsylvania 19380

Dedication

Dedicated to the memory of my grandfather, William H. Leeks, who gave me the first of many drugstore memories.

Published by Schiffer Publishing, Ltd.
1469 Morstein Road
West Chester, Pennsylvania 19380
Please write for a free catalog.
This book may be purchased from the publisher.
Please include $2.00 postage.
Try your bookstore first.

Price Guide included

Copyright © 1991 by Schiffer Publishing, Ltd.
Library of Congress Catalog Number: 91-65649.

Printed in the United States of America.
ISBN: 0-88740-334-4

We are interested in hearing from authors with book ideas on related topics.

Ceramic and metal Cherry Chic dispenser, J. Hungerford Smith Co., Rochester, New York. The crock is marked "ATCo." *Courtesy of the House of Stuart.*

Acknowledgments

The idea for this book arose during a visit to John and Elsie Booker's store in Chapel Hill, North Carolina. Called Patterson's Mill Country Store, it is a fascinating place, recreating the charm of the country store, which in itself is worthy of a visit. But in two of the side rooms is recreated the corner drugstore of the early 1900s, complete with all the medicines, paraphernalia and atmosphere one would expect to find. John and Elsie allowed us to invade their store to capture it on film. It took several days, and they were there with information and assistance. John even took all the glass off the displays so we could get at the shelves. Since then they have been a constant encouragement as the book inched its way toward completion. I thank them.

We received the same hospitality at the Hook's Historic Drugstore and Pharmacy Museum on the grounds of the State Fair in Indianapolis, Indiana. Tom Dingledy of Hook's Drugs said yes to our request, and Marion Poehler, the curator of the museum, gave up a day off to open the store to us and give us access to their fine collection. Again, we thank them for making this book possible.

Along the way others have opened their collections and shops to us. We appreciate their generosity. They include: Betty Blair, Apple Attic, Jackson, Ohio; Renee Braverman, R.A.G. Time, New York, New York; Frank & Betty Lou Gay; Ron Koehler & Cindy Marsh, Koehler Bros. Inc.-The General Store, Lafayette, Indiana; Gary Metz, Muddy River Trading Company, Roanoke, Virginia; and Don Stuart, House of Stuart, Jinsen Beach, Florida.

Some of these contacts were made possible by Neal Wood of L & W Books who graciously invited us to two national advertising shows in Indianapolis, where some of the leading dealers in antique advertising gather twice each year. He gave us the space and the introductions that made our job enjoyable and easy.

Bob Biondi and Kate Dooner of the Schiffer team were of great assistance in gathering information and photography. Ellen J. (Sue) Taylor brought her skill and artistry to the design of the book.

Part of the satisfaction of creating a book, such as this, is the opportunity to make new friends. Those who have contributed their objects to this endeavor have also given a little of themselves. Thank you.

Douglas Congdon-Martin
West Chester, Pennsylvania

Porcelain apothecary jars. The two on the left are marked Rexall on the back, indicating their use in that franchise. The other two are similar enough to make one wonder if they are part of the same group, but different enough to leave it open to question. 12" tall. *Courtesy of Koehler Bros. Inc.—The General Store, Lafayette, Indiana.*

HOLLISTER PHARMACY
CIGARS • PRESCRIPTIONS A SPECIALTY • ICE CREAM SODA
SATIN
SATIN SKIN FACE POWDER
FREE TO YOU
COME INSIDE AND GET
TWO BOXES
SATIN SKIN POWDER
SATIN
SATIN
SATIN SKIN CREAM
FREE TO YOU
COME INSIDE AND GET
TWO BOXES
SATIN SKIN POWDER
SATIN
SATIN
SATIN
SATIN
SATIN

Contents

The soda jerk at his post in this old drug store, circa 1920.

Brass Pharmacy sign in the form incorporating the letter A and the mortar and pestle. 28.5" x 16". *Courtesy of the House of Stuart.*

Introduction

Among my earliest memories is that of accompanying my grandfather to the corner drugstore. A visit to my grandparent's home was not complete without a walk to Kaplan's Drugstore, which was located about a block away, at the corner of Jefferson Ave. and Algonquin, on the east side of Detroit. Usually we went to pick up a box of Banker's Choice cigars or a remedy for the current ache or pain. Sometimes we just stopped in for a Coke or an ice cream soda.

The drugstore was, for me, what the general store was for my country cousins. On its shelves it seemed to have almost every imaginable thing. They teemed with remedies, candies, toys, gadgets, and tobacco. Advertisements plastered the walls and every available inch of counter space. Their bright colors and strong images appealed even to one who could not read their messages of miraculous cures and comforts.

No words were needed with wooden mortar and pestle telling the observer that they were passing a pharmacy. 18" x 11.5". *Courtesy of John & Elsie Booker, Patterson's Mill Country Store, Chapel Hill.*

At the center of my memory is the soda fountain, that wonderful place. Grandfather would lift me up on the tall stool with the revolving seat. I usually could get at least one spin in before I was told to behave myself, but even while behaving myself I would constantly move back and forth.

Behind the bar was the soda jerk, in his white jacket and little paper cap. He was the master of sweets, and I remember envying his job. To have ready access to all that ice cream and soda pop was a child's dream. I watched his every move. First, he carefully set the paper liner in the silver holder, then he folded back the heavy doors of the ice cream chest revealing the treasures inside. With the scoop rinsed in warm water to help it cut through the hard packed ice cream he would reach deeply into the chest, sometimes to the point where I thought he would fall in, and come up with a heaping serving of rich, dark chocolate ice cream. By adding a scoop of marshmallow cream, a swirl of whipped cream, and a cherry he created a culinary delight.

While the soda fountain assured that the drugstore would keep a place in my memory for a lifetime, the important thing about this neighborhood institution was something less tangible. This was a place where people met and exchanged the news and rumors of the day. This was a place where compassion was dispensed along with medicine, where healing took place in spirit as well as body. Like the country store in America's rural life, the drugstore was the center of the city neighborhood, the hub around which its life revolved.

The importance of the neighborhood drugstore has led to an interest in its artifacts among today's collectors. From apothecary jars to fountain syrup dispensers, patent medicines to baby bottles, tobacco to mortars and pestles, the products, advertising, and paraphernalia of America's drugstores is avidly sought after and collected. In addition to those who specialize in drugstore and soda fountain collectibles, the broad range of their merchandizing covers many other collections as well: tobacco tins, advertising, bottles, coin ops, and country store collectibles.

Whatever interest you bring to this book, we hope you find something of value in these pages. The purpose of this book is to explore the variety and beauty of these objects. We hope it will lead to a renewed and deepened appreciation.

Early interior shots of Hook's Drug Stores in Indianapolis, Indiana, c. 1931. The stores were located at 101 Pennsylvania, Penn and Washington, and on Washington Street. *Courtesy of Hook's Historic Drug Store and Pharmacy Museum, Indianapolis.*

Die-cut cardboard fan advertising Lee's Drug Store, Natrona Heights, Pennsylvania. C.W. Carson Co., 11" x 8". *Courtesy of Koehler Bros. Inc.—The General Store, Lafayette, Indiana.*

This beautiful reverse painted and gilded sign in a copper and brass frame once hung at the Court Square Drug Company in Durham, North Carolina. 47.25" x 20.5". *Courtesy of John & Elsie Booker, Patterson's Mill Country Store, Chapel Hill.*

1908 calendar for Yearby's Drug Store, Durham and Edgemont, North Carolina. 11" x 9". *Courtesy of John & Elsie Booker, Patterson's Mill Country Store, Chapel Hill.*

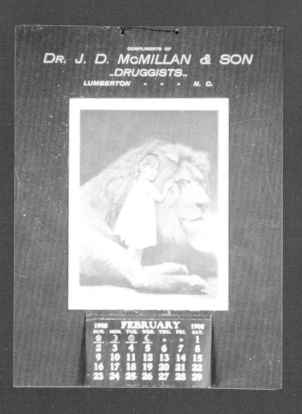

1908 calendar for J.D. McMillan & Sons Druggists, Lamberton, North Carolina. Woodman & Tierman Printing, St. Louis. 13" x 10". *Courtesy of John & Elsie Booker, Patterson's Mill Country Store, Chapel Hill.*

INTERIORS

John & Elsie Booker run the Patterson Mill Country Store in Chapel Hill, North Carolina. Part of the store is set aside for an extensive Pharmacy Museum. It reflects Mrs. Booker's love of her profession and dedication to preserving its history. She was one of the first women to be registered as a pharmacist in North Carolina. The front room of the pharmacy has the counter for waiting on people with its impressive array of apothecary jars. *Courtesy of John & Elsie Booker, Patterson's Mill Country Store, Chapel Hill.*

It also has a fountain area, which was an important tool for bringing customers into the store. *Courtesy of John & Elsie Booker, Patterson's Mill Country Store, Chapel Hill.*

Opposite page:
The back room was the pharmacist's domain where prescription medicines were kept and processed. *Courtesy of John & Elsie Booker, Patterson's Mill Country Store, Chapel Hill.*

I. The Stores

Stepping over the threshold of an early drugstore took one into a wondrous, mysterious world. One was bombarded by a sensory explosion of sight, sound, and taste.

The eyes were dazzled by a burst of color. The shelves teemed with bright candy sticks and ball gum. From the ceiling were suspended display jars filled with colored water, a traditional symbol of the pharmacy. The walls were lined boxes and bottles of the patent medicines, perfumes, and soaps and powders, many of them featuring the latest marvels of chromolithography. Closer to the pharmacist's work area were row upon of row of apothecary jars. Most were of glass filled with powders and crystals of various colors. Others were made of porcelain with beautiful decorations. Behind all this color, and making it more vivid by contrast, were the rich, dark woods of the cabinetry, highlighted by mirrors, reverse painted

glass, and the bright advertising of the drug companies. When all this was taken together, the effect was kaleidoscopic, delighting and exciting to the eye.

The nose also tingled with the drugstore experience. A veritable bouquet of odors and scents filled the place. At the front of the store one encountered the chocolate mists rising from the soda fountain. A little further back, the musty smell of tobacco competed with the musky fragrances of the perfume counter. Finally, as one neared the pharmacist's work area, the aroma of ammonia, carbonic acid, and iodoform took over the senses. Reminiscing on his youth in his father's drugstore, Richard Armour, who had the job of cleaning perfume beakers and scouring the utensils of the pharmacist, reports that, "when the wind was right, my mother did not need to look out the window. She knew I was on my way home when I was still half a block away."[1]

And there were the tastes, some good, some bad. The good tastes were immediate. These included the ice creams, sodas, sandwiches, and other treats one ate at the fountain. And one could never go to the drugstore without feeding the sweet tooth at the candy counter, with its large and varied selection. The bad tastes were delayed, saved for home consumption, which probably kept the drugstore relatively free from association with the agonies of castor oil or the other nostrums that lined the shelves. While these sometimes were made to be flavorful, more often than not they were bitter and unappealing. It would take a heap of ice cream to counteract the taste of one teaspoon of patent medicine.

In the time before self-service, the drugstore was usually lined with high shelves and cupboard space around its walls. In front of the shelves there was an aisle for the clerks. They waited on customers from behind long counters, which were often made of glass to reveal the treasures within. Always they were covered with displays and counter advertisements to entice the customer to buy a little extra.

The fountain would be near the door, where it would serve as an attraction to passers-by. A few stools would be at the bar, and there may be two or three parlor tables with chairs around them.

At the back of the store was a closed off area where the druggist prepared prescriptions. The pharmacist's work area was the inner sanctum of the drugstore. It was there that the pharmacist worked to create miracles from the jars of powders, herbs, and chemicals that lined the shelves of the drugstore. It was a miniature laboratory with test tubes, beakers, mortars and pestles, great copper distillers and percolators, and scales so sensitive they had to be encased in glass so that the air would not make them inaccurate.

Armour remembers the pharmacist's work area not only as a laboratory, but also as the helm of a ship. "Here my father...like the captain...seemed to be navigating perilous seas, now and then peering through a tiny porthole to see what was going on up forward."[2]

For the uninitiated, the pharmacist's work was as mysterious as that of the ancient alchemist, and he or she was held in similar esteem in the community. Like the alchemist, the pharmacist was able to decipher the cryptic messages that the doctors placed on their prescription forms. Often the handwriting was so bad it could easily be mistaken for a code. Then from Latin-labeled jars he would take the precise amounts to create the medication the doctor ordered.

With a scarcity of medical doctors, the pharmacist often became the "Doc" of first resort. When people came down with the flu or a cold they went to "Doc" to get some potion that would make them well, or at least make them feel better. If they received a cut or other injury their first instinct was not to go to the hospital, but to the pharmacist. The druggist was a learned person, whose opinion could be trusted and who was accessible to those in need.

It is easy to see why the drugstore became a center of the community's life. The sense of well-being and good cheer that emanated from its walls and people encouraged healing and hope. Many early stores even had a pot bellied stove around which people could gather for support, comfort, and warmth.

Common to most early pharmacies was the pot bellied stove and lots of cabinet space. *Courtesy of John & Elsie Booker, Patterson's Mill Country Store, Chapel Hill.*

From the overall view of the Hook's Pharmacy, with its pot-bellied stove in the middle, it is easy to see why early pharmacies became the center of the neighborhood. The octagonal structure at the back of the room is the pharmacist's work area, seen below. *Courtesy of Hook's Historic Drug Store & Pharmacy Museum, Indianapolis.*

The work area was designed to have the supplies and equipment the pharmacist needed close at hand, and to provide a window for watching the store. *Courtesy of Hook's Historic Drug Store & Pharmacy Museum, Indianapolis.*

13

The fountain and candy area also play an important role at the Hook's Antique Pharmacy on the Indiana State Fair Grounds in Indianapolis. *Courtesy of Hook's Historic Drug Store & Pharmacy Museum, Indianapolis.*

It is still possible to buy some items at the Hook's Antique Pharmacy. *Courtesy of Hook's Historic Drug Store & Pharmacy Museum, Indianapolis.*

The beautifully done cabinetry in the Hook's Antique Pharmacy combines walnut, etched glass, and reversed painted glass for a beautiful effect. *Courtesy of Hook's Historic Drug Store & Pharmacy Museum, Indianapolis.*

A swinging door that separated the pharmacist's work area from the sales floor. Wood with leaded glass panel, 64" x 25". *Courtesy of Koehler Bros. Inc.—The General Store, Lafayette, Indiana.*

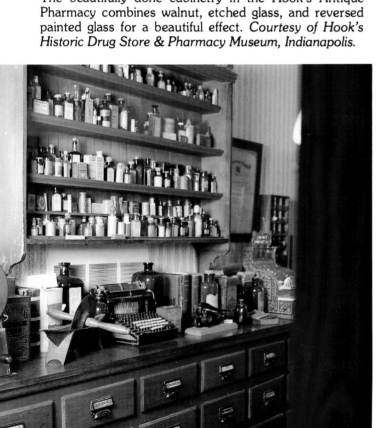

Behind the pharmacist were more storage areas and other necessary equipment. *Courtesy of Hook's Historic Drug Store & Pharmacy Museum, Indianapolis.*

Wooden table for the Myer Drug Co., 30" x 15" x 15". Painted logo. *Courtesy of Koehler Bros. Inc.—The General Store, Lafayette, Indiana.*

15

TOOLS OF THE TRADE
GENERAL

The typewriter was a part of almost every pharmacist's work space. This Remington is 10.5" x 15.5". *Courtesy of John & Elsie Booker, Patterson's Mill Country Store, Chapel Hill.*

In the pharmacies of the late-1800s and up until today, one of the most important business tools was the telephone. Not only was it a way of customer contact, it also saved many lives that were endangered by a doctor's handwriting. *Courtesy of John & Elsie Booker, Patterson's Mill Country Store, Chapel Hill.*

To free their hands, pharmacists used prescription holders like this cast iron one. 5" high. *Courtesy of Hook's Historic Drug Store & Pharmacy Museum, Indianapolis.*

A label dispenser like this held labels for the pharmacy, as well as preprinted labels for many of the more common prescription drugs. Wood and metal, 27" x 16". *Courtesy of John & Elsie Booker, Patterson's Mill Country Store, Chapel Hill.*

A simple wire prescription holder. 4.5" x 2.75". *Courtesy of John & Elsie Booker, Patterson's Mill Country Store, Chapel Hill.*

This Bates Perforator, Model 2, was used to punch a hole in the prescription record for storage. Bates Mfg. Co., Orange, New Jersey. 6.5" x 6.25". *Courtesy of John & Elsie Booker, Patterson's Mill Country Store, Chapel Hill.*

The perforated prescription records were slipped onto a wire, which hung in the pharmacist's work area for easy reference. *Courtesy of John & Elsie Booker, Patterson's Mill Country Store, Chapel Hill.*

17

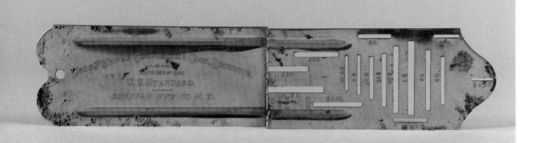

The pharmacist also needed to be a business person, and several companies were ready to help. This Gold & Silver Counterfeit Coin Detector was patented February 27, 1877 by the Berrian Mfg. Co., New York. Steel, 2" x 9.75". *Courtesy of Hook's Historic Drug Store & Pharmacy Museum, Indianapolis.*

Most purchases in the drugstores were wrapped in paper and tied with a string from a cast iron string dispenser like this. 8" x 6". *Courtesy of Hook's Historic Drug Store & Pharmacy Museum, Indianapolis.*

The pharmacists required accurate measurements both of weight and volume. Their work area always included a good balancing scale like the marble example. On the front is a dial with arrows which align when a balance is reached. On the back is the seal of the Department of Weights and Measures. *Courtesy of John & Elsie Booker, Patterson's Mill Country Store, Chapel Hill.*

This cast iron scale by Ohaus has porcelain on steel platforms. 6″ x 14″. *Courtesy of John & Elsie Booker, Patterson's Mill Country Store, Chapel Hill.*

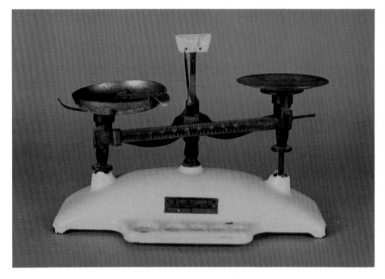

A balance scale with enameled base and weight holder, and a removable platform for convenient pouring. The Levitt-Ferguson Co., Baltimore, Maryland. 5.75″ x 10″. *Courtesy of John & Elsie Booker, Patterson's Mill Country Store, Chapel Hill.*

The counter weight scale is by Fairbanks and has the Fairbanks Standard logo on its marble platform piece. Cast iron, 8.75″ x 20″. *Courtesy of John & Elsie Booker, Patterson's Mill Country Store, Chapel Hill.*

Class X Weights by Christian Becker, Inc., New York came in a wooden box with a metal clasp. 1.25″ x 3.75″ x 2″. *Courtesy of John & Elsie Booker, Patterson's Mill Country Store, Chapel Hill.*

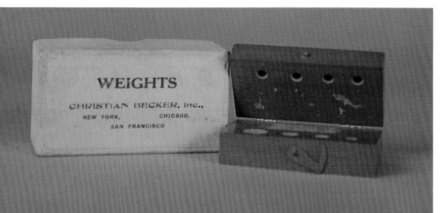

Dr. C. H. Fitch's Prescription Scale has the counter weight design and can fold into the small box for transport into the field. Patented 1885. 3" long. *Courtesy of Hook's Historic Drug Store & Pharmacy Museum, Indianapolis.*

This wood, brass and marble scale is designed for accuracy. It has adjustment screws to make it level, and a glass cover the covers the weighing mechanism to keep the air currents out. Henry Troemner, Philadelphia, Pennsylvania. 8" x 13.25". *Courtesy of John & Elsie Booker, Patterson's Mill Country Store, Chapel Hill.*

In the laboratory the pharmacist made use of a variety of glassware, some of it quite beautiful in form. Funnels came in a variety of sizes and designs. These range from 6" to 8". *Courtesy of John & Elsie Booker, Patterson's Mill Country Store, Chapel Hill.*

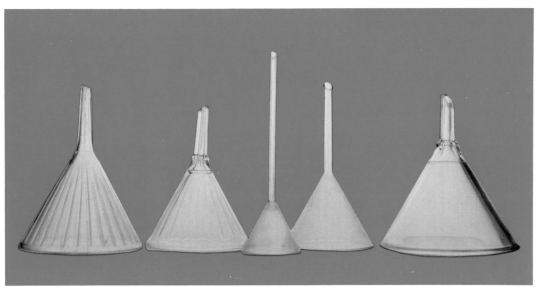

Graduated beakers saw a lot of use in the pharmacy. These range from 6-8 inches. *Courtesy of John & Elsie Booker, Patterson's Mill Country Store, Chapel Hill.*

This group gives an idea of the variety of shapes of the beakers. 3"-6.25". *Courtesy of John & Elsie Booker, Patterson's Mill Country Store, Chapel Hill.*

Still other sizes and shapes of beakers, these were smaller and used for finer measurements. 2.75"-5". *Courtesy of John & Elsie Booker, Patterson's Mill Country Store, Chapel Hill.*

Assorted beakers, flasks, and pipettes commonly used in the pharmacist's work. 1.25"—6". *Courtesy of John & Elsie Booker, Patterson's Mill Country Store, Chapel Hill.*

Three types of storage jars. On the left is a bell jar of heavy glass and designed to sit over something to keep it protected. In the center are two museum jars with a mechanism which screws down to keep the top secure. On the right is a counter display jar, designed as much for beauty as for its storage function. 6"—11". *Courtesy of John & Elsie Booker, Patterson's Mill Country Store, Chapel Hill.*

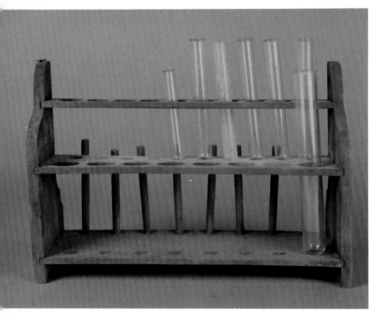

Test tubes and rack. 7" x 10". *Courtesy of John & Elsie Booker, Patterson's Mill Country Store, Chapel Hill.*

Chemists stand and glass funnels. 24" tall. *Courtesy of Hook's Historic Drug Store & Pharmacy Museum, Indianapolis.*

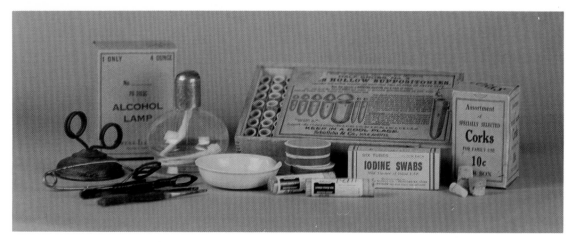

A variety of pharmacist's equipment including, from left to right: a brass and steel prescription holder by Albert Rich, Chicago; test tube holders and tweezers; an alcohol lamp and its box, Owens-Illinois; a porcelain dish; Schieffelin hollow suppositories made of Butter of Cacao; and an assortment of corks. *Courtesy of John & Elsie Booker, Patterson's Mill Country Store, Chapel Hill.*

Still in use today, suppositories were once an even more common means of delivering medication. They came hollow as in the previous example so that they could be filled with the drug of choice. They also came ready-to-use like the Urethral Suppositories in this example by the John Wyeth & Brother Company in Philadelphia. The pharmacists had the ability to make their own using molds like those shown here. These were usually brass and came in a variety of sizes. *Courtesy of Hook's Historic Drug Store & Pharmacy Museum, Indianapolis.*

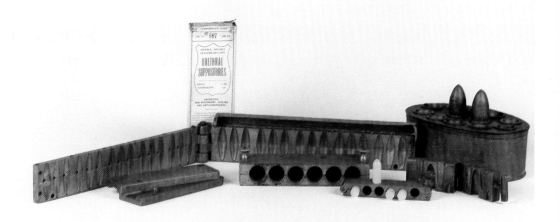

To fill the molds the pharmacist could use a suppository compactor such as these. Left to right: The Arthur Remedy Co, 7" x 11" 2"; Archibalds, Pat'd 1879, 9" x 5" x 2"; Unmarked, 7" x 5" x 2". Cast iron. *Courtesy of Hook's Historic Drug Store & Pharmacy Museum, Indianapolis.*

Pharmacists also made their own pills following the prescribed formula. This "piping board" by V.W. Brinckerhoff was used to create long strands of a drug mixture that could then be uniformly cut into tablets. The brass plates came in different sizes to make pills of different diameters. Wood and brass, 2" x 16" x 6". Originated with Dr. Robert M. Fuller, 1878. *Courtesy of John & Elsie Booker, Patterson's Mill Country Store, Chapel Hill.*

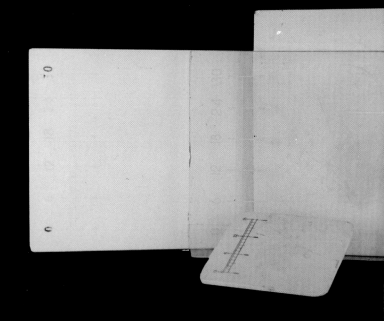

The strings of medicine were laid on a graduated cutting tray like these to assure the accurate and uniform sizing of the tablets as they were being cut. They were usually made in marble or glass. These measure from 6" x 6" to 12" x 12". *Courtesy of Hook's Historic Drug Store & Pharmacy Museum, Indianapolis.*

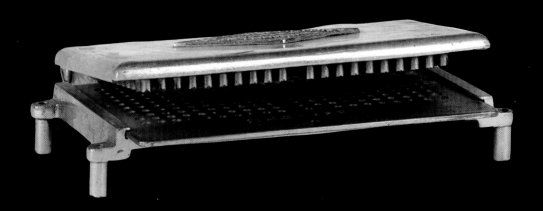

A tablet triturate used for "mass producing" tablets. Arthur Colton, Detroit, Michigan. 3" x 9" x 7.5". *Courtesy of Hook's Historic Drug Store & Pharmacy Museum, Indianapolis.*

A somewhat more complicated tablet triturate by Colton. 5″ x 11″ x 6″. *Courtesy of Hook's Historic Drug Store & Pharmacy Museum, Indianapolis.*

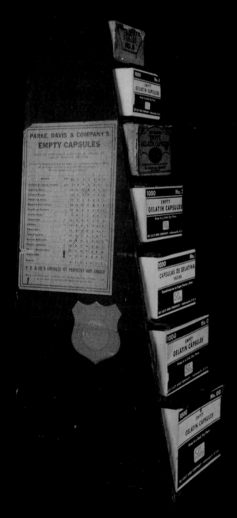

Parke, Davis & Company produced empty capsules which the pharmacist could fill as necessary. This graduated stand holds several different sizes. *Courtesy of John & Elsie Booker, Patterson's Mill Country Store, Chapel Hill.*

The use of leeches for the treatment of various conditions goes back hundreds of years, and has experienced something of a resurgence in recent times. This ceramic container was used by the pharmacist to keep them until they were needed. 9″ x 6″. *Courtesy of Hook's Historic Drug Store & Pharmacy Museum, Indianapolis.*

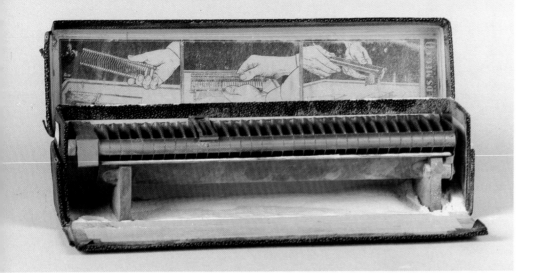

Another form medicine took was as a powder. This powder paper machine by the Child's Mfg. Co., El Dorado, Kansas, was used to create the proper dosage of powder. The powder was placed in paper (see below) to be given to the customer. Metal, 2.25" x 10". *Courtesy of Hook's Historic Drug Store & Pharmacy Museum, Indianapolis.*

Powder papers by Eli Lilly and Company, Indianapolis. The sheets measured 4.25" x 5.75". *Courtesy of John & Elsie Booker, Patterson's Mill Country Store, Chapel Hill.*

Spatulas used for counting pills and trays were often given to the pharmacists by the drug companies heavily marked with the companies' advertising. *Courtesy of John & Elsie Booker, Patterson's Mill Country Store, Chapel Hill.*

Opposite page bottom left:
Every child's worst nightmare, Castor Oil, was kept in bulk by the pharmacist and dispensed via a castor oil pump like this one. 29" x 11" x 11". *Courtesy of John & Elsie Booker, Patterson's Mill Country Store, Chapel Hill.*

For the salves and ointments pharmacists used dispensing tanks like this Phenix by Whitall Tatum Company, New York. *Courtesy of John & Elsie Booker, Patterson's Mill Country Store, Chapel Hill.*

A copper distiller used in the pharmacy. 17" x 24". *Courtesy of Hook's Historic Drug Store & Pharmacy Museum, Indianapolis.*

Another copper distiller would have rubber or copper tubing attached to the peak. 25.5″ x 22″ x 11″. *Courtesy of Hook's Historic Drug Store & Pharmacy Museum, Indianapolis.*

An emulsifier from the 1890s. Ceramic and iron, 12″ x 10″. *Courtesy of Hook's Historic Drug Store & Pharmacy Museum, Indianapolis.*

Two percolators used for brewing medicinal teas. Left: plated tin; right: porcelain. 8.25″ x 5″. *Courtesy of Hook's Historic Drug Store & Pharmacy Museum, Indianapolis.*

Copper boilers used to keep things warm. The various rings could be inserted to accommodate different sized objects. Left: 6.5″ in diameter; right: 5″ in diameter. *Courtesy of Hook's Historic Drug Store & Pharmacy Museum, Indianapolis.*

Atomizers. *Courtesy of Hook's Historic Drug Store & Pharmacy Museum, Indianapolis.*

Though the mortar and pestle is the most commonly associated grinding tool of the pharmacist, there have been others. This grinder was used in the early 19th century, and is cleverly designed to use both the wheel and gravity to accomplish its task. Wood and iron, 20″ long. *Courtesy of Hook's Historic Drug Store & Pharmacy Museum, Indianapolis.*

A grinder by M.J. Jones, Pennyan, New York, "Inventor & Manufacturer." Patented May 17, 1887. Wood and tin, 18.5″ x 9″ x 14.5″. *Courtesy of Hook's Historic Drug Store & Pharmacy Museum, Indianapolis.*

Cork presses were used to turn raw cork into the proper size to stop prescription bottles. This one is cast iron, 7.5″ long, and can make four different sizes. *Courtesy of Hook's Historic Drug Store & Pharmacy Museum, Indianapolis.*

While today we are rightly concerned about toxic waste and its disposal, it was not of particular concern to the early pharmacist. This is a glass waste bottle in a wooden frame. Where it was taken when filled is anybody's guess. 27″ x 12″ x 2″. *Courtesy of Hook's Historic Drug Store & Pharmacy Museum, Indianapolis.*

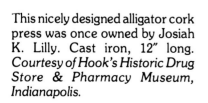

This nicely designed alligator cork press was once owned by Josiah K. Lilly. Cast iron, 12″ long. *Courtesy of Hook's Historic Drug Store & Pharmacy Museum, Indianapolis.*

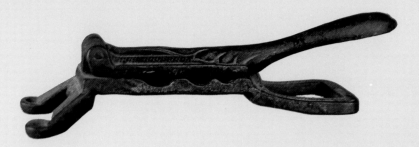

Cork press with three sizes. 10" x 2.5". *Courtesy of John & Elsie Booker, Patterson's Mill Country Store, Chapel Hill.*

Cork press, three sizes. 10" x 3.25". *Courtesy of John & Elsie Booker, Patterson's Mill Country Store, Chapel Hill.*

Cork press marked on the top with the letter M in a diamond. 2.75" x 9.5". *Courtesy of John & Elsie Booker, Patterson's Mill Country Store, Chapel Hill.*

A heavy duty Yankee cork press, 6" x 13". *Courtesy of John & Elsie Booker, Patterson's Mill Country Store, Chapel Hill.*

Cork press, 3" x 11.5". *Courtesy of John & Elsie Booker, Patterson's Mill Country Store, Chapel Hill.*

Early pill case, 10.5" x 8". This was used by physicians to carry their medicines into the homes. *Courtesy of Hook's Historic Drug Store & Pharmacy Museum, Indianapolis.*

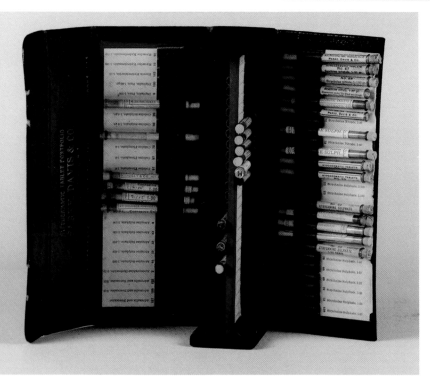

Hydrodermatic Tablet Portfolio from Parke, Davis, & Co., Detroit. These vials contained tablets that could be dissolved in water and injected into a patient. *Courtesy of Hook's Historic Drug Store & Pharmacy Museum, Indianapolis.*

MORTARS AND PESTLES

Very early Egyptian mortar, c. 1000 B.C. Stone, 4.5″ x 5.5″. *Courtesy of Hook's Historic Drug Store & Pharmacy Museum, Indianapolis.*

Bronze mortars and pestle from the late 15th century. The vertical ribs are typical of the early Gothic mortars. France, 3″ x 4″. *Courtesy of Hook's Historic Drug Store & Pharmacy Museum, Indianapolis.*

Bronze mortar and pestle from Italy, 16th century. The squat shape indicates it is of Roman origin. The vertical "ribs" have evolved into Medusa heads, indicating that the mortar may be of the late Gothic period. 3.75″ x 5.25″. *Courtesy of Hook's Historic Drug Store & Pharmacy Museum, Indianapolis.*

This bronze mortar and pestle is from the Netherlands, c. 1590, and is indicative of a transition piece. The handles and rings encircling the mortar are Gothic; the decoration is typically Renaissance. It bears the inscription "Leefte verwint al dinks": "Faith overcomes all things." 3.75″ x 4″. *Courtesy of Hook's Historic Drug Store & Pharmacy Museum, Indianapolis.*

A covered mortar inscribed with various dates from 1839-1880. Bronze, 4.25" x 6.5". *Courtesy of Hook's Historic Drug Store & Pharmacy Museum, Indianapolis.*

Handled brass mortar and pestle, 4" x 4". *Courtesy of John & Elsie Booker, Patterson's Mill Country Store, Chapel Hill.*

A group that shows the variety of forms and materials used in mortars and pestles. *Courtesy of Hook's Historic Drug Store & Pharmacy Museum, Indianapolis.*

Mortar and pestle, brass, 3" x 4.5". *Courtesy of John & Elsie Booker, Patterson's Mill Country Store, Chapel Hill.*

Brass mortar and pestle, 2.75″ x 3″. *Courtesy of John & Elsie Booker, Patterson's Mill Country Store, Chapel Hill.*

Mortar and pestle, cast iron, 5.5″ x 6.5″. *Courtesy of John & Elsie Booker, Patterson's Mill Country Store, Chapel Hill.*

Handled brass mortar and pestle, 4″ x 4.25″. *Courtesy of John & Elsie Booker, Patterson's Mill Country Store, Chapel Hill.*

Well-used cast iron mortar and pestle, 8″ x 9″. *Courtesy of John & Elsie Booker, Patterson's Mill Country Store, Chapel Hill.*

Cast iron mortar and pestle, 4″ x 4″. *Courtesy of John & Elsie Booker, Patterson's Mill Country Store, Chapel Hill.*

Nice black marble mortar and pestle, 5.5" x 4.5". *Courtesy of John & Elsie Booker, Patterson's Mill Country Store, Chapel Hill.*

Tapering marble mortar and pestle, 4.5" x 2.75". *Courtesy of John & Elsie Booker, Patterson's Mill Country Store, Chapel Hill.*

Nice green marble mortar and pestle, 4.75" x 5.5". *Courtesy of John & Elsie Booker, Patterson's Mill Country Store, Chapel Hill.*

Vase-shaped marble mortar and pestle, 7.5" x 6". *Courtesy of John & Elsie Booker, Patterson's Mill Country Store, Chapel Hill.*

White marble mortar and pestle, 4.5" x 4". *Courtesy of John & Elsie Booker, Patterson's Mill Country Store, Chapel Hill.*

This wooden mortar and pestle has seen a lot of use. 4" x 6". *Courtesy of John & Elsie Booker, Patterson's Mill Country Store, Chapel Hill.*

A handsome walnut mortar with a maple pestle. 7" x 5". *Courtesy of John & Elsie Booker, Patterson's Mill Country Store, Chapel Hill.*

Five glass footed mortars and pestles. 2.25" x 4". *Courtesy of John & Elsie Booker, Patterson's Mill Country Store, Chapel Hill.*

A hand-carved oak mortar and pestle, 6.5" x 6.5". *Courtesy of Hook's Historic Drug Store & Pharmacy Museum, Indianapolis.*

Bowl-shaped ceramic mortar without lip, 2.5″ x 5″.

Someone cared enough to add a little decoration to this mortar and pestle. Wood, 7″ x 6″. *Courtesy of John & Elsie Booker, Patterson's Mill Country Store, Chapel Hill.*

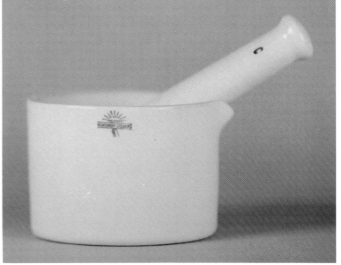

For practical, everyday use during the last fifty years or more, the predominant materials have been ceramic and glass. This lipped cylindrical mortar is by Winthrop Stearn, 3.25″ x 4.75″. *Courtesy of John & Elsie Booker, Patterson's Mill Country Store, Chapel Hill.*

A bowl-shaped ceramic mortar with lip, 3″ x 5″.

An ointment mill used to grind powders for ointment preparations. Glass, 4.5" tall x 3.75" diameter at the base. *Courtesy of Hook's Historic Drug Store & Pharmacy Museum, Indianapolis.*

Schering-Coricidin mortar and pestle in bronzed metal honoring Pharmacy Fraternities. 3" x 3". *Courtesy of John & Elsie Booker, Patterson's Mill Country Store, Chapel Hill.*

Schering-Coricidin has created a number of commemorative mortars and pestles which they used as promotionals with pharmacies. In 1982 they celebrated their twentieth in the series, so we assume that they began in 1962. This bronzed metal piece commemorates Louis J. Dufilmo, Jr., America's first licensed pharmacist, 1816, and Pharmace Francaise Pharmacy Museum. 2.5" x 2.5". *Courtesy of John & Elsie Booker, Patterson's Mill Country Store, Chapel Hill.*

Mortar and pestle honoring Joseph Price Remington, 1847-1918. Schering-Coricidin, 4.25" x 4". *Courtesy of John & Elsie Booker, Patterson's Mill Country Store, Chapel Hill.*

Coricidin mortar and pestle honoring Pedanios Dioscorides, circa 77 A.D. Bronzed metal, 4″ x 5″. *Courtesy of John & Elsie Booker, Patterson's Mill Country Store, Chapel Hill.*

Mortar and pestle honoring Stanislas Limousin, pharmacal inventor, 1831-1867. Schering, 4.5″ x 3.25″. Bronzed metal. *Courtesy of John & Elsie Booker, Patterson's Mill Country Store, Chapel Hill.*

Schering mortar & pestle, bronzed metal, 4″ x 4.75″. *Courtesy of John & Elsie Booker, Patterson's Mill Country Store, Chapel Hill.*

Pedestal mortar commemorating the First Pharmacy, 1752. Bronzed metal, 4.25″ x 4.25″. *Courtesy of John & Elsie Booker, Patterson's Mill Country Store, Chapel Hill.*

Pottery mortar (mug?) honoring Calen, 131-201 A.D. Coricidin, 3.75″ x 4″. *Courtesy of John & Elsie Booker, Patterson's Mill Country Store, Chapel Hill.*

1969 Coricidin commemorative mortar and pestle remembering Louis Hebert, 1580-1627. Pottery and wood, 4.5″ x 5″. *Courtesy of John & Elsie Booker, Patterson's Mill Country Store, Chapel Hill.*

Bronzed metal mortar commemorating Dr. John Morgan, 1735-1789. Coricidin, 4″ x 4.75″. *Courtesy of John & Elsie Booker, Patterson's Mill Country Store, Chapel Hill.*

Bronzed metal Cosmas & Damian mortar and pestle. Schering, 4.75″ x 4.5″. *Courtesy of John & Elsie Booker, Patterson's Mill Country Store, Chapel Hill.*

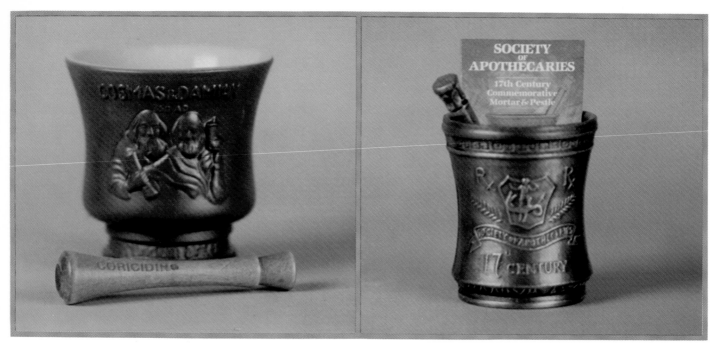

A very similar mortar to the one above, except in pottery with a wooden pestle. Schering, 5″ x 5″. *Courtesy of John & Elsie Booker, Patterson's Mill Country Store, Chapel Hill.*

The 20th mortar and pestle in Schering-Coricidin's series was issued in 1982. Bronzed metal, 4.25″ x 3.75″. *Courtesy of John & Elsie Booker, Patterson's Mill Country Store, Chapel Hill.*

The bicentennial mortar and pestle came in two sizes. The large one is 4″ x 5″, the small one is 3″ x 3″. Coricidin, 1976. Bronzed metal. *Courtesy of John & Elsie Booker, Patterson's Mill Country Store, Chapel Hill.*

APOTHECARY JARS
Early

Five early apothecary jars, pre-1850. These are hand-blown with colorful paper labels, and glass stoppers. 3.5" tall. *Courtesy of John & Elsie Booker, Patterson's Mill Country Store, Chapel Hill.*

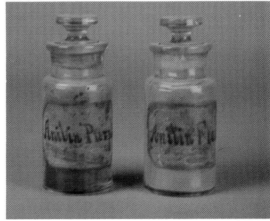

Hand-blown apothecary jars with paper labels, pre-1850. 4" tall. *Courtesy of John & Elsie Booker, Patterson's Mill Country Store, Chapel Hill.*

Five early hand-blown apothecary jars, pre-1850. Paper labels and glass stoppers. 4.5" tall. *Courtesy of John & Elsie Booker, Patterson's Mill Country Store, Chapel Hill.*

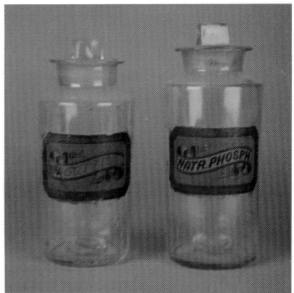

Wide-mouthed hand-blown apothecary jars with glass stoppers, pre-1850. 7.5" tall. *Courtesy of John & Elsie Booker, Patterson's Mill Country Store, Chapel Hill.*

Three large hand-blown glass apothecary jars, pre-1850. Paper labels, 9.5" tall. *Courtesy of John & Elsie Booker, Patterson's Mill Country Store, Chapel Hill.*

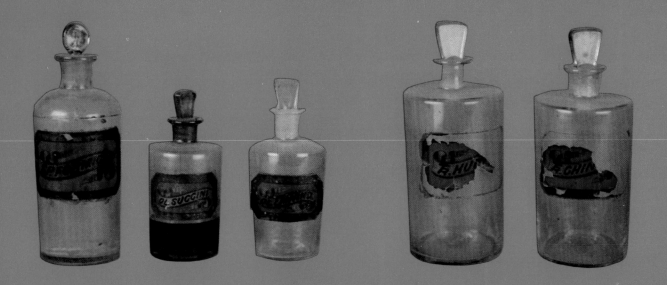

An assortment of early hand-blown glass apothecary jars, 5.25″—7.5″. *Courtesy of John & Elsie Booker, Patterson's Mill Country Store, Chapel Hill.*

8″ tall hand-blown glass apothecary jars, pre-1850. Narrow mouthed, with paper labels. *Courtesy of John & Elsie Booker, Patterson's Mill Country Store, Chapel Hill.*

Round Jars with Narrow Mouths

Three decorative apothecary jars. The two footed jars on the left are by W.R. Warner & Co., Philadelphia, and were patented September 8, 1875. Their labels are gilded and reverse painted, and they are applied without being recessed. The one on the right is engraved with festoons and "Biddle's Satisfaction Bouquet." It has a reverse painted glass label. The tallest of the three is 9″. *Courtesy of John & Elsie Booker, Patterson's Mill Country Store, Chapel Hill.*

Somewhat unusually designed round apothecary jar with cork stopper, c. 1880. 9.5″ tall. *Courtesy of John & Elsie Booker, Patterson's Mill Country Store, Chapel Hill.*

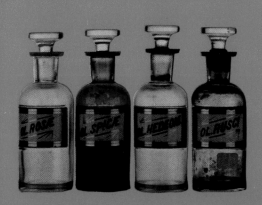

Narrow-mouthed apothecary jars with gilded reverse painted glass labels recessed, c. 1890. 6″ tall. *Courtesy of John & Elsie Booker, Patterson's Mill Country Store, Chapel Hill.*

Round narrow-mouthed glass apothecary jars with gilded and reverse painted labels, c. 1875. The labels are not recessed. 10″ tall. *Courtesy of John & Elsie Booker, Patterson's Mill Country Store, Chapel Hill.*

Four large glass apothecary jars with narrow mouths and recessed glass labels, c. 1890. 10.75″ tall. *Courtesy of John & Elsie Booker, Patterson's Mill Country Store, Chapel Hill.*

Glass apothecary jars with narrow mouths and recessed reverse painted glass labels. 9″ tall. *Courtesy of John & Elsie Booker, Patterson's Mill Country Store, Chapel Hill.*

Large wide-mouthed apothecary jars, c. 1875. The gilded and reversed painted labels are not recessed on the four jars on the left, but the jar on the right has a recessed label.

Wide mouthed apothecary jars with applied gilded glass labels, not recessed. Circa 1880, 10″ tall. *Courtesy of John & Elsie Booker, Patterson's Mill Country Store, Chapel Hill.*

Wide-mouthed apothecary jar with glass oval label applied, but not recessed, c. 1880. 10″ tall. *Courtesy of John & Elsie Booker, Patterson's Mill Country Store, Chapel Hill.*

Eight wide-mouthed round apothecary jars, c. 1890. 5.25" tall with glass recessed labels. *Courtesy of John & Elsie Booker, Patterson's Mill Country Store, Chapel Hill.*

Six wide-mouthed (and one narrow mouthed) apothecary jars, c. 1890. Recessed glass labels, 7" tall. *Courtesy of John & Elsie Booker, Patterson's Mill Country Store, Chapel Hill.*

Square Jars with Narrow Mouths

Narrow-mouthed apothecary jars with ribbed stoppers. 10.25" tall. *Courtesy of John & Elsie Booker, Patterson's Mill Country Store, Chapel Hill.*

A pretty group of square apothecary jars. Recessed reverse painted labels with gilding, c. 1890. *Courtesy of Hook's Historic Drug Store & Pharmacy Museum, Indianapolis.*

Square Wide-Mouthed

Five wide-mouthed apothecary jars, including an amber one, all c. 1890. Recessed reverse painted glass labels. 10.25″ tall. *Courtesy of John & Elsie Booker, Patterson's Mill Country Store, Chapel Hill.*

Wide-mouthed apothecary jars, c. 1890. Note the unusual red label on one of them. The labels are reverse painted glass and recessed. 10″ tall. *Courtesy of John & Elsie Booker, Patterson's Mill Country Store, Chapel Hill.*

Other Glass Apothecaries

A variety of 10″ glass apothecary jars, c. 1890. The one on the left has a paper label, the others are reversed painted on glass and recessed. *Courtesy of John & Elsie Booker, Patterson's Mill Country Store, Chapel Hill.*

An assortment of glass apothecary jars, 8.5 inches high. *Courtesy of John & Elsie Booker, Patterson's Mill Country Store, Chapel Hill.*

Four French Limoges apothecary jars used to hold crude drugs. These rather large jars, 16" x 7", are quite beautiful. *Courtesy of Hook's Historic Drug Store & Pharmacy Museum, Indianapolis.*

Tubes with dried herbs and plants for use in medicines. Packaged by Emberg Pharmacy, Campello, Massachusetts. 6" x 1.25". *Courtesy of John & Elsie Booker, Patterson's Mill Country Store, Chapel Hill.*

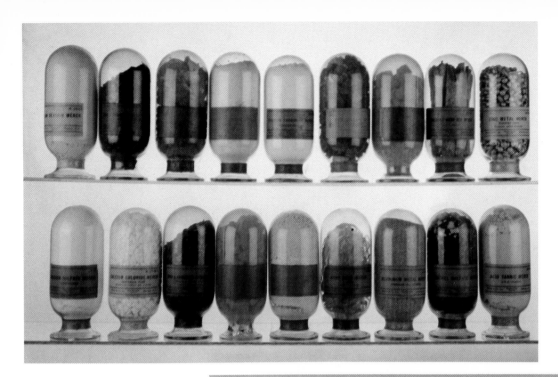

Display jars with raw drugs. While these drugs could have been used by the pharmacist, one suspects that they were more for show than use. Merck Laboratories. 4.75" tall.

Despite the ravages of time and use, these reverse painted glass apothecaries, hold onto some of their former beauty. 11" tall x 6" in diameter. *Courtesy of Hook's Historic Drug Store & Pharmacy Museum, Indianapolis.*

Three beautiful old blue-gray porcelain apothecary jars with applied labels, c. 1850. 11" tall. *Courtesy of Hook's Historic Drug Store & Pharmacy Museum, Indianapolis.*

51

Opal apothecary jars used for creams and ointments. The jars on the ends have (had) reversed painted glass labels. The middle jar has the name incised. *Courtesy of John & Elsie Booker, Patterson's Mill Country Store, Chapel Hill.*

Glass apothecary jars with paper labels. The taller one is dated 1893 and marked Whitall Tatem & Co., New York. Tall: 16″; short: 10″. *Courtesy of John & Elsie Booker, Patterson's Mill Country Store, Chapel Hill.*

Tin raw drug containers from Parke, Davis & Company. These six are representative of the many that Parke, Davis manufactured for use by pharmacists. The lithographed tin canister has a place for a label describing the contents. 9″ x 5″ x 5″. *Courtesy of John & Elsie Booker, Patterson's Mill Country Store, Chapel Hill.*

An apothecary-like jar used at the Fulgham Pharmacy, Fountain City, Indiana for Prussian Blue Dye. Blown glass, 7.5" tall, c. 1870. *Courtesy of Hook's Historic Drug Store & Pharmacy Museum, Indianapolis.*

Graduated prescription bottles came in a variety of sizes. *Courtesy of John & Elsie Booker, Patterson's Mill Country Store, Chapel Hill.*

Amber glass ointment jar, 6.5" x 4.5". *Courtesy of Koehler Bros. Inc.—The General Store, Lafayette, Indiana.*

Three cobalt jars marked Frank E. Morgan & Sons, Philadelphia. 4.25"—7". *Courtesy of John & Elsie Booker, Patterson's Mill Country Store, Chapel Hill.*

PRESCRIPTION DRUGS

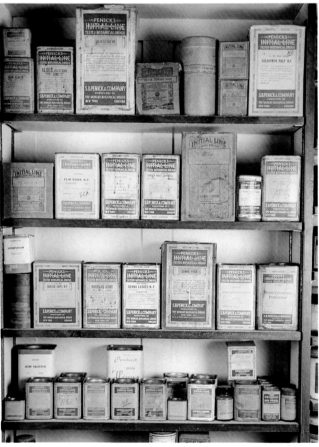

A more recent version of the apothecary jar was the amber glass bottle, with a paper label, although some traces of the older jars can be seen in the designs of the labels. *Courtesy of John & Elsie Booker, Patterson's Mill Country Store, Chapel Hill.*

Bottles line the shelves of the pharmacist's work area, containing everything from powdered placenta and pituitary gland to opium and lactated pepsin. *Courtesy of John & Elsie Booker, Patterson's Mill Country Store, Chapel Hill.*

Crude drugs from several companies fill the pharmacist's drawers, including Parke, Davis and Company, Detroit, Allaire Woodward & Co., Peoria, Illinois, S.W. Gould & Bros. Botanic Garden, Malden, Massachusetts, and Sharp & Doehme, Baltimore, Maryland.

Crude drugs of various kinds. S.B. Penick & Co. of New York packaged most of these. *Courtesy of John & Elsie Booker, Patterson's Mill Country Store, Chapel Hill.*

Gilbert Bros. & Co. of Baltimore sent their Laudanum in wooden boxes like this one. The lithography was done by Maryland Lith. Co., Baltimore. *Courtesy of John & Elsie Booker, Patterson's Mill Country Store, Chapel Hill.*

One way to collect pharmaceutical items is to focus on a certain store and collect what is available. Some of the history of this company can be seen in this group with Haywood & Boone Prescription Druggists of Durham, North Carolina, becoming Boone Drug Co., The Prescription Pharmacy. *Courtesy of John & Elsie Booker, Patterson's Mill Country Store, Chapel Hill.*

Another item in the pharmacist's repertoire may have been this balsam apple in whiskey, used for the treatment of colds. The bottle is F.G. Tullidge Old Windsor Whiskey, Cincinnati, Ohio. *Courtesy of Hook's Historic Drug Store & Pharmacy Museum, Indianapolis.*

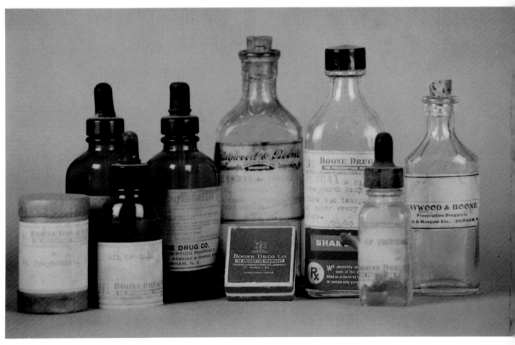

Prescription bottles, c. 1900 from John Hook's first drugstore in Indianapolis. *Courtesy of Hook's Historic Drug Store & Pharmacy Museum, Indianapolis.*

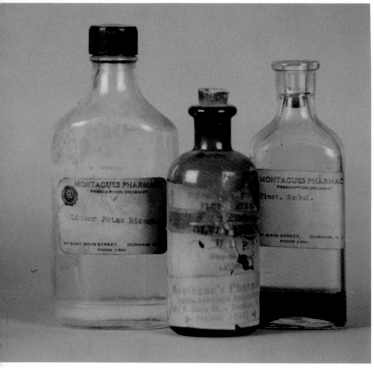

Bottles from Montague's Pharmacy, Durham. *Courtesy of John & Elsie Booker, Patterson's Mill Country Store, Chapel Hill.*

Three containers from the W.H. King Drug Co., Raleigh, North Carolina. *Courtesy of John & Elsie Booker, Patterson's Mill Country Store, Chapel Hill.*

Promotional jewelry. The cuff-links and tie jewelry is from Schering. *Courtesy of John & Elsie Booker, Patterson's Mill Country Store, Chapel Hill.*

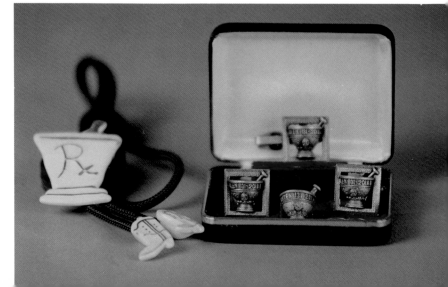

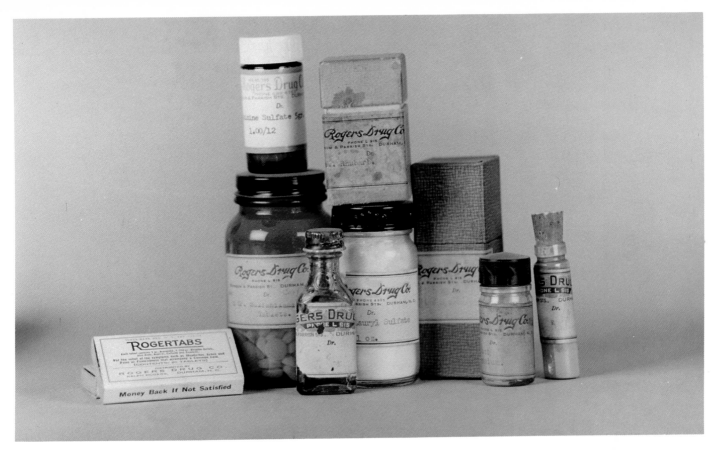

Products of the Rogers Drug Co., Durham, North Carolina. Druggists were always trying to find formulas that would find a larger market in the patent medicine realm. Here you see Rogertabs, a formula for headaches. *Courtesy of John & Elsie Booker, Patterson's Mill Country Store, Chapel Hill.*

The drug manufacturers used give-aways to promote their products. The best of these were useful tools that would put the company name in front of the pharmacist day after day. *Courtesy of John & Elsie Booker, Patterson's Mill Country Store, Chapel Hill.*

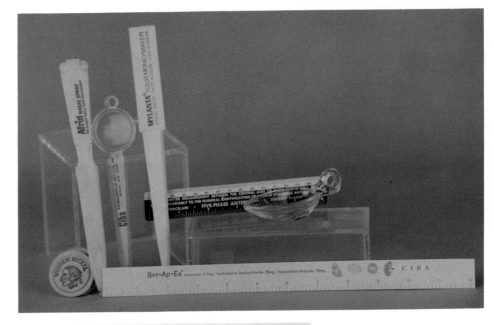

Brightly decorated promotional glasses, c. 1960s. 5" tall. *Courtesy of John & Elsie Booker, Patterson's Mill Country Store, Chapel Hill.*

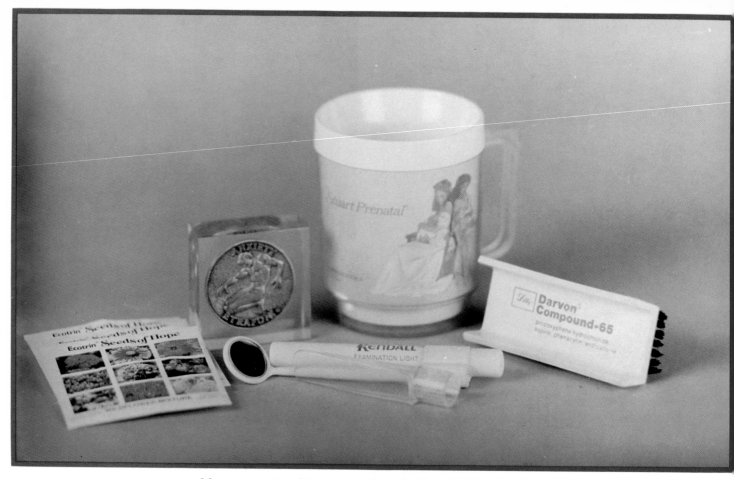

More promotional items including the Ecotrin "Seeds of Hope." *Courtesy of John & Elsie Booker, Patterson's Mill Country Store, Chapel Hill.*

Alchemists symbol for sulfur given as a promotion for Tinactin by Schering. 4.5″ x 2.75″. *Courtesy of John & Elsie Booker, Patterson's Mill Country Store, Chapel Hill.*

Promotional glasses with an etched Rx. *Courtesy of John & Elsie Booker, Patterson's Mill Country Store, Chapel Hill.*

II. The Soda Fountain

While one tends to think of the early drugstore and the soda fountain as two parts of a whole, it was not always so. Richard Armour remembers the resistance his traditionally minded father had to placing a fountain in their drugstore. "My father...was an old-time druggist, and to him a soda fountain had no more place in a drugstore than a pool table in a bank."[3]

Armour continues: "'I don't care if they net two hundred dollars a month,' my father said, though he did care... 'I'm running a drugstore, not an ice cream parlor. Do you know what you get when you put in a soda fountain? You get riffraff sitting around sucking five-cent sodas for an hour and using up half a dozen free straws. Or you get lovesick kids drinking one soda between them. You get people with the nerve to come in and ask for a drink of water. You get syrup spots on the floor. You get ants."

Armour's father was not alone in his opinion of soda fountains. In his "Boosting Business" column in the April, 1920 issue of *Drug Topics*, John Todd Somerset bemoans "certain good folks in the drug trade with a bias for the ways of the days agone." In fact, he said the proof of the benefits of soda fountains were abundant, conclusive, and eloquent. "...The soda fountain is the most valuable, most useful, most profitable, and altogether most beneficial business building feature assimilated by the drug store in a generation. ..The wonder is that any druggist in a desirable location, in the face of present pyramiding taxes and overhead, likewise the increased demand for soft drinks resulting from prohibition, can fail to see which way the wind is blowing and the trout running and become a soda fan quick!"

Somerset cites the success of the soda fountain at the Liggett's Drugstore in Grand Central Station to prove his point. Arguably the busiest store in America in 1920, some 12,000 people each day passed through its doors. Of this, some 8,000 came primarily to patronize the soda fountain. "Visualize for a second, brother, what this soda business means," Somerset wrote.

"Eight thousand glasses of soda a day means 2,920,000 glasses a year. Figure eight ounces to the glass, these 2,920,000 glasses, placed end to end, would stretch 389 miles, from Chicago to Milwaukee...Measure by volume, they represent 23,360,000 ounces, 182,523 gallons, 36 tons, or enough to float a super-dreadnought [a heavily armed battleship]."

When you add to this the sandwiches, cakes, pies, doughnuts, coffee, and tea, it is easy to see the contribution that the soda fountain made to the drugstore. Then when you consider the other things they would buy on impulse, the contribution was even bigger. In 1920, "when a dollar was a dollar" and a sandwich cost from 10 to 25 cents each, it was estimated that the fountain at Grand Central Station brought in $500,000 dollars each year, with a net profit of 33%.

Summarizing his argument for the soda fountain, Somerset wrote:

"The answer seems simple.

"Soda dispensing is dignified, clean cut, wholesome and altogether desirable, making for health, comfort, happiness and a sense of good cheer. It conserves all that is good, moral and righteous in the community, stimulates sociability as distinguished from conviviality, exerts a sobering influence and provides a meeting place from folks, young and old, with whom you desire to become acquainted for the other business they may bring you.

"The bar is dead, the fountain lives, and soda is king!"

Sun Shine Seltzer bottles, St. Petersburg, Florida. 11" x 3.5". *Courtesy of John & Elsie Booker, Patterson's Mill Country Store, Chapel Hill.*

THE FOUNTAIN AND ITS EQUIPMENT

Marble and brass soda dispenser. *Courtesy of Hook's Historic Drug Store & Pharmacy Museum, Indianapolis.*

Opposite page:
This soda fountain at Hook's Antique Pharmacy makes it easy to see why people were attracted to them. *Courtesy of Hook's Historic Drug Store & Pharmacy Museum, Indianapolis.*

Candy was always available at the soda fountain for that insatiable sweet tooth. *Courtesy of Hook's Historic Drug Store & Pharmacy Museum, Indianapolis.*

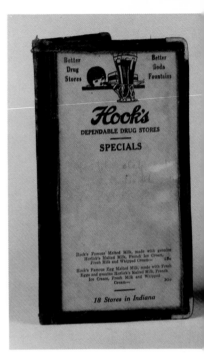

Pepsi Cola glasses. 5″ tall. *Courtesy of Koehler Bros. Inc.—The General Store, Lafayette, Indiana.*

Four De-Lux Cola glasses, 4″ tall. *Courtesy of John & Elsie Booker, Patterson's Mill Country Store, Chapel Hill.*

Fountain glasses, 5.5″—6.75″. *Courtesy of John & Elsie Booker, Patterson's Mill Country Store, Chapel Hill.*

Ten ounce Pepsi-Cola glasses, 5.25″ tall. *Courtesy of Koehler Bros. Inc.—The General Store, Lafayette, Indiana.*

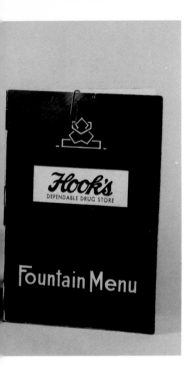

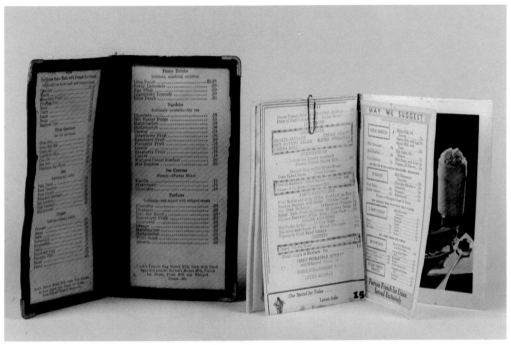

Hook's Pharmacy fountain menus. Though they are undated they show a hint of deco in their cover design and the prices on the inside suggest the 1920s and 1930s. The taller menu is simply for fountain items with Cokes for a nickel and strawberry sundaes for fifteen cents. The other menu is more complete. The Green Plate special for the day includes smoked sausage, cream gravy, hot potato, salad, sliced pineapple and a Vienna roll for twenty-five cents. *Courtesy of Hook's Historic Drug Store & Pharmacy Museum, Indianapolis.*

Plate from St. John's Fountain. Syracuse China, Econo Rim™, 5.5" in diameter. *Courtesy of Koehler Bros. Inc. — The General Store, Lafayette, Indiana.*

Six four-inch Coca-Cola glasses. *Courtesy of John & Elsie Booker, Patterson's Mill Country Store, Chapel Hill.*

Four Coca-Cola glasses, 5" tall. *Courtesy of John & Elsie Booker, Patterson's Mill Country Store, Chapel Hill.*

Heinz Juice glasses, 5″ tall. *Courtesy of Koehler Bros. Inc.—The General Store, Lafayette, Indiana.*

Borden's Elsie the Cow ice cream cups. Glass, 4″ x 3.5″. *Courtesy of Koehler Bros. Inc.—The General Store, Lafayette, Indiana.*

Assorted cup holders. The end holders are by Lily and
measure 3.5″ x 6″. The shorter holder is Dixie, No. 8727,
made in Easton, Pennsylvania, 4″ x 2.5″. The tall thin Vortex
holder dates from the 1920s, and is 2.75″ x 4″. *Courtesy of
John & Elsie Booker, Patterson's Mill Country Store,
Chapel Hill.*

Benedict Indestructo silverplated, silver soldered fountain
cups. 6.5″ x 3″. *Courtesy of Koehler Bros. Inc.—The
General Store, Lafayette, Indiana.*

Thompson Double Malted Malted Milk shaker. Aluminum,
7″ x 3.5″. *Courtesy of Koehler Bros. Inc.—The General
Store, Lafayette, Indiana.*

Silverplated fountain ice cream cups by Benedict Indestructo. 5" x 4". *Courtesy of Koehler Bros. Inc.—The General Store, Lafayette, Indiana.*

Silverplated sundae insert holders, 4.5" x 5". *Courtesy of Koehler Bros. Inc.—The General Store, Lafayette, Indiana.*

Four ounce Hemo Thompson Double Malted Malted Milk with Beef and Iron shakers. Stainless steel, 4" x 3". *Courtesy of John & Elsie Booker, Patterson's Mill Country Store, Chapel Hill.*

Glass fountain ware. Shaker, 8.5"; Strawholder, 11"; Cruet, 9". *Courtesy of John & Elsie Booker, Patterson's Mill Country Store, Chapel Hill.*

Milk shake maker and two ice cream scoops. The shake maker is nickel plated brass, 15" tall. The small scoop is 7" long by Nevco, Japan. The larger scoop is marked Rainbow and is 10.25" long. *Courtesy of Betty Lou and Frank Gay.*

C.C. Clawson's Snow King Ice Shaver. Cast iron, 20" x 19" x 8". *Courtesy of John & Elsie Booker, Patterson's Mill Country Store, Chapel Hill.*

Juicers. *Courtesy of John & Elsie Booker, Patterson's Mill Country Store, Chapel Hill.*

Box of 500 10.5" paper straws from Pepsi, c. 1950s. Paper, 11" x 4" x 4". *Courtesy of John & Elsie Booker, Patterson's Mill Country Store, Chapel Hill.*

Seltzer bottles by the Sparklets Corporation, New York. 14" x 4.5". *Courtesy of John & Elsie Booker, Patterson's Mill Country Store, Chapel Hill.*

Fountain ware in use at Hook's Antique Pharmacy in Indianapolis.

Ice cream cone holder. *Courtesy of Hook's Historic Drug Store & Pharmacy Museum, Indianapolis.*

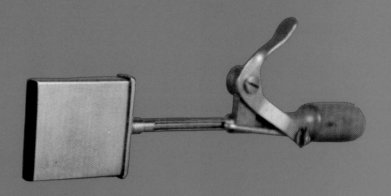

Scoop for ice cream to make ice cream sandwiches. 12" x 3.5". *Courtesy of Betty Lou and Frank Gay.*

Assorted mechanical ice cream scoops of brass and wood. 10" long. *Courtesy of Betty Lou and Frank Gay.*

Key wind ice cream scoops. The largest scoops are 4" deep. The others are 3.5" and 3" respectively. *Courtesy of Betty Lou and Frank Gay.*

SYRUP AND OTHER DISPENSERS

Lash's California Orangeade syrup dispenser. 13″ tall. *Courtesy of John & Elsie Booker, Patterson's Mill Country Store, Chapel Hill.*

Orange Crush syrup dispenser, glass and cast iron, 18″ x 7″. *Courtesy of Gary Metz.*

Triple XXX Cola syrup dispenser, manufactured by Hall. Crockery, 12″ x 7″. *Courtesy of Gary Metz.*

Superior Iced Tea dispenser. Ceramic, 11″ x 8.5″. *Courtesy of Koehler Bros. Inc.—The General Store, Lafayette, Indiana.*

Rare Indian Rock Ginger Ale syrup dispenser. Ceramic, 15" x 7.5". Courtesy of Gary Metz.

Buckeye Root Beer ceramic syrup dispenser, The Cleveland Fruit Juice Co., 14.5″ x 8″. *Courtesy of Gary Metz.*

The ruby glass portion of a Fowler's Cherry Smash syrup dispenser. 8″ x 7″. *Courtesy of Koehler Bros. Inc.—The General Store, Lafayette, Indiana.*

October Sweet Apple Cider dispenser with all original parts. Stoneware, 13″ x 9″. *Courtesy of Betty Blair.*

Oak and steel Liggett Root Beer Barrel, 19″ x 13.5″. *Courtesy of Koehler Bros. Inc.—The General Store, Lafayette, Indiana.*

Glass Heinz Juice dispenser, 16″ x 8″ x 8″. *Courtesy of Koehler Bros. Inc.—The General Store, Lafayette, Indiana.*

Maybon Orange True cooler and dispenser. A ceramic liner which held ice fit into the top of this tin dispenser. 10" x 15". *Courtesy of John & Elsie Booker, Patterson's Mill Country Store, Chapel Hill.*

Hot Soda fountain of brass, manufactured and guaranteed by Manning, Bowman and Co., Meriden, Connecticut. The water in the samovar was heated and added to one of syrups neatly stored on the surrounding rack. The "Hot Soda" sign is on a pivot and may have been set in motion by the rising heat. 40" tall. *Courtesy of Betty Lou and Frank Gay.*

Crockery dispenser with an insert to hold ice as a coolant. 13" x 10". *Courtesy of Hook's Historic Drug Store & Pharmacy Museum, Indianapolis.*

Coca-Cola syrup bottle. 12" x 3.5". *Courtesy of John & Elsie Booker, Patterson's Mill Country Store, Chapel Hill.*

Though similar to the Hot Soda fountain above, the shelf of this samovar is too short for syrup bottles. It was more likely used for more traditional purposes like hot water for tea or coffee. The container on the back contained the fuel. Copper and brass, 32.5" x 16". *Courtesy of R.A.G. Time.*

Another beautiful piece, this copper warmer served a dual purpose. First, and most importantly it was a double boiler to keep fudge and other ice cream toppings warm. Secondly, hot water could be drawn as needed through the spigot. *Courtesy of Hook's Historic Drug Store & Pharmacy Museum, Indianapolis.*

Borden's Malted Milk display jar, glass with a tin top. 9" x 6". *Courtesy of Gary Metz.*

Aluminum Thompson's Malted Milk display container, from the Birk Pharmacy in Indianapolis, which closed in 1918. 10" x 6.25". *Courtesy of Hook's Historic Drug Store & Pharmacy Museum, Indianapolis.*

Horlick's Malted Milk tin. Racine, Wisconsin, 6.5" x 7". *Courtesy of John & Elsie Booker, Patterson's Mill Country Store, Chapel Hill.*

Large Carnation Malted Milk tin. 13" x 9.5" x 9.5". *Courtesy of John & Elsie Booker, Patterson's Mill Country Store, Chapel Hill.*

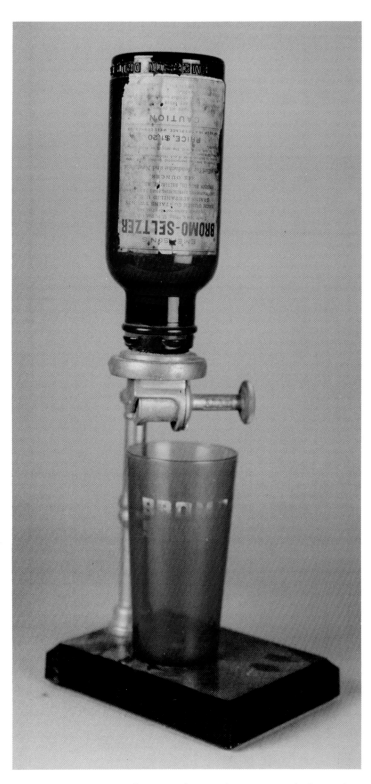

That a prominent feature of many drugstore soda fountains was the Bromo-Seltzer dispenser, was probably not a comment on the food. Bromo-Seltzer was started by Isaac Emerson in Chapel Hill, North Carolina. Metal and glass with a porcelain base. *Courtesy of John & Elsie Booker, Patterson's Mill Country Store, Chapel Hill.*

A somewhat later Bromo-Seltzer dispenser, 8.5" tall. *Courtesy of John & Elsie Booker, Patterson's Mill Country Store, Chapel Hill.*

A large Mello-Freeze tin, c. 1937. 11.75″ x 7″. *Courtesy of John & Elsie Booker, Patterson's Mill Country Store, Chapel Hill.*

...on syrup bottle from the Powers-Taylor Drug Co.,
..., sent to Vinson's Pharmacy, Halifax, North
...Tin and wood, 15″ x 8″. *Courtesy of John & Elsie*
...atterson's Mill Country Store, Chapel Hill.

Oak Pepsi-Cola barrel. 13″ x 19.5″. *Courtesy* ...
Elsie Booker, Patterson's Mill Country Store, ...

...t Beer Extract, enough to make 40 pint
...x 1.5″. *Courtesy of John & Elsie Booker,*
...Mill Country Store, Chapel Hill.

FOUNTAIN ADVERTISING

Electrified Coca-Cola fountain sign. Brass and glass, 14" x 12.5" x 5". *Courtesy of Gary Metz.*

Triangular Coca-Cola sign with pierced fret work. Wood with metal, the Coke bottle is raised applied wood. 17" x 20". *Courtesy of John & Elsie Booker, Patterson's Mill Country Store, Chapel Hill.*

Coca-Cola sign, c. 1954. Snyder & Black Litho, New York. 27" x 16". *Courtesy of John & Elsie Booker, Patterson's Mill Country Store, Chapel Hill.*

Tin Cherry Smash sign, 9" in diameter. *Courtesy of John & Elsie Booker, Patterson's Mill Country Store, Chapel Hill.*

1937 Orange Crush sign on cardboard. 19" x 12". *Courtesy of John & Elsie Booker, Patterson's Mill Country Store, Chapel Hill.*

Tin Coca-Cola thermometer. 15.75" x 6.75". *Courtesy of John & Elsie Booker, Patterson's Mill Country Store, Chapel Hill.*

Cardboard sign for Grapette Soda. Consolidated Litho Corporation, Brooklyn, New York, 25″ x 18″. *Courtesy of John & Elsie Booker, Patterson's Mill Country Store, Chapel Hill.*

Hanging cardboard fountain signs. Lemons, 10.5″ x 5″; Way Up, 5″ x 7″, Cherry Blossom, 8.75″ x 6″. *Courtesy of John & Elsie Booker, Patterson's Mill Country Store, Chapel Hill.*

"Fresh up with 7-Up" paper counter advertisement, c. 1949. 8″ x 5″. *Courtesy of John & Elsie Booker, Patterson's Mill Country Store, Chapel Hill.*

Embossed tin sign for Buffalo Rock Ginger Ale. 13.5″ x 9.5″. *Courtesy of John & Elsie Booker, Patterson's Mill Country Store, Chapel Hill.*

PATENT MEDICINES

Assorted products of the Atlas Medicine Co., Henderson, North Carolina. *Courtesy of John & Elsie Booker, Patterson's Mill Country Store, Chapel Hill.*

Products of the Astypodyne Chemical Company and the Apinol Corporation, both of Wilmington, North Carolina. *Courtesy of John & Elsie Booker, Patterson's Mill Country Store, Chapel Hill.*

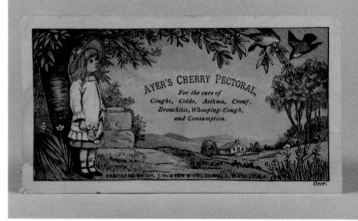

Ayer's Cherry Pectoral trade card, Dr. J.C. Ayer & Co., Lowell, Massachusetts. Two-sided paper, 2.5″ x 5″. *Courtesy of Hook's Historic Drug Store & Pharmacy Museum, Indianapolis.*

Enamel sign for Base Ball Liniment and IBP laxative, Pearson Remedy Co., Burlington, North Carolina. 12″ x 26″. *Courtesy of John & Elsie Booker, Patterson's Mill Country Store, Chapel Hill.*

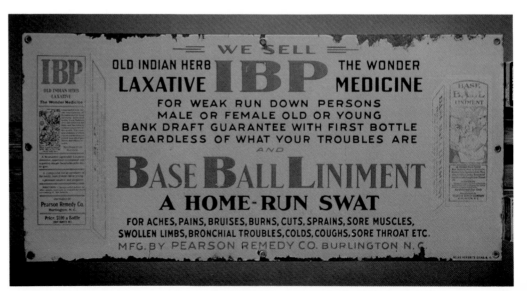

III. The Products

What was most interesting about the old drugstore, and continues to be fascinating about the new, is the shear variety and number of products one could find on its shelves. Like its country store cousin, the drugstore carried a little bit of everything.

Taking up the bulk of the shelf space were hundreds of patent medicines. Americans have long been susceptible to the promise of a wonder drug, a miraculous elixir that could cure what ails them. In the years before the Pure Food and Drugs Act of 1906, there was little to limit the kinds of concoctions that could be labeled as medicine and advertised to the public. The patent potions included everything from innocuous colored water to dangerous combinations of poisons and heavy metals like mercury. They were purported to cure nearly every illness known to humankind, both real and imagined.

The first remedies arrived in America from England, at least as early as 1708. In the *Boston News-Letter* for October 1 of that year there was an advertisement for "DAFFY'S Elixir Salutis, very good, at four shillings and six-pence per half pint bottle."[4] Customers were eager for these remedies both in the colonies and the mother land. A list of other English medicines that found their way across the Atlantic appeared in the Pennsylvania Gazette in 1768 and included "Anderson's, Hooper's, and Lockyer's pills, Bateman's drops, British oil, Bostock's, Squires, and Daffey's elixirs, Stoughton's bitters, Turlington's balsam of life,

Dr. James fever powders, Godfrey's cordial."[5] Most of these were patented in England and were either drawn from or adopted by the more orthodox practitioners of medicine.

America was hooked on patent medicines. In his excellent study of the history of patent medicines, *Toadstool Millionaires: A Social History of Patent Medicines in America before Federal Regulations,* James H. Young reports that the American Revolution spurred a trend that had begun in the middle of the 1700s: bottling English medicines in America. Until the revolutionary tensions stopped all trade, empty bottles for the various medicines would be imported and filled here. The reputable apothecaries would replicate the English formulae, while the less than honorable would create some formula of their own. With the cessation of trade, apothecaries and counterfeiters alike took to refilling used bottles.[6]

The bottle was of critical importance to the marketing of the product. In an age of wide-spread illiteracy, it was the bottle that distinguished one medicine from another. Indeed, in America, very few medicines were actually patented. To do so meant revealing the formula, and that was an important secret. Instead, companies patented the uniquely shaped bottles that held their medicines. They also copyrighted the labels and promotional pieces, and patented trademarks that assured their rights while not requiring them to reveal any trade secrets.[7]

The drugs in the drugstore were not only for humans. Barker made animal medicines that were commonly carried in pharmacies. These paper boxes are for their Horse and Cow Medicinal, 7.25" x 4.73", and the Poultry Powder, 6.25" x 4". Barker, Moore, & Meis Co., Philadelphia, Pennsylvania. *Courtesy of John & Elsie Booker, Patterson's Mill Country Store, Chapel Hill.*

This Barker liniment was "For Man or Beast." Wood, 7.25" x 7.5". *Courtesy of John & Elsie Booker, Patterson's Mill Country Store, Chapel Hill.*

The laxness in the law meant that anyone from the local druggist to the parson to the milk man could develop and market a remedy, and during the 1800s many tried. They took old family recipes, folk medicine cures, and mixtures of their own design, bottled them and put them up for sale. Success depended more upon marketing savvy than the powers of the potions. Many failed, some managed to gain a local market, and a few, with particular genius, went on to capture a national market and become what Oliver Wendell Holmes called "toadstool millionaires," a phrase which Young borrowed for the title of his excellent study.

One might wonder how these medicines made it to the drugstore shelves. Often they contained large proportions of alcohol, opiates, and other ingredients that were, at best, unproven and, at worst, deadly. Other medicines contained nothing at all, save for a little coloring or flavor mixed in water. The danger in these latter drugs was that they kept people from seeking medical help. So, what were they doing in the drugstore?

The simple answer is that the people wanted them. The patent drug companies were the pioneers in establishing brand names through advertising. They were so effective in getting people to ask for their products by name, that drugstores could not afford to be without them. If they did not carry a particular patent medicine, their customers would simply go elsewhere, to another drugstore, the general store, or the traveling salesperson.

Besides their genius in advertising, the makers of patent medicines also benefitted from the state of medicine in the mid-1800s. People were desperate for a simple cure. Medical science was very little advanced from the middle ages. The findings of Lister and Pasteur about the nature of illness were yet to come, and physicians resorted to the therapies of blood letting, purging, and surgery to treat most diseases. Young traces this "heroic" medicine to the patriot doctor Benjamin Rush and his followers. "Throughout the country Rush's disciples deliberately bled the ill to unconsciousness—and now and then to death—and prescribed such tremendous doses of calomel that patients lost teeth and even jawbones."[8]

There was, of course, much resistance to these radical treatments, and doctors were held in very low esteem. People would try anything else before going to the doctor. The makers of patent medicine played upon this attitude in every advertisement, every promotional they devised, and they were numerous. One advertisement for Spence's Positive Powders had two panels. The first, labeled "The Old Way of Doctoring the Sick" shows a miserable woman being cared for by a nurse, with a caption that read:

"Nurse: Well, Mrs. Fogy, the Doctor's Ipecac vomits you splendidly. We will soon give you the Calomel and Jalap, next the Castor Oil, then an injection, and after that we will apply the blister and the leeches, and if necessary shave your head. You will be well in three or four weeks,—a little salivated, perhaps, but that's nothing. The Doctor won't charge you more than $40 or $50."

The second panel is labeled "The New Way of Curing the Sick," and shows a woman sitting comfortably in bed taking tea and toast, while her husband watches in amazement.

"Husband: What, Mary, well already, and eating toast and tea! I left you with a raging fever this morning.

"Wife: Yes, Albert, I am well already, and I took nothing but six of Spence's Positive Powders. They acted like a charm, and they cost only two cents and a half a piece. That is the tiniest doctor's bill you ever paid."[9]

The appeal is obvious, and the manufacturers spent millions of dollars to get their message across, and to insure that the public would recognize and remember their name. They incorporated beautiful design with a message that their elixir would cure dozens of common ailments, and some not so common. They peppered the advertisements with testimonials about the cures, and the people believed them.

In addition to prescription drugs and patent medicines, drugstores were the place to find other "necessities of life." Every store had a large area dedicated to tobacco products. They carried cigars, smoking and chewing tobacco, and snuff, along with the pipes and papers that were necessary to enjoy them.

The Booker Laboratories in Norfolk, Virginia produced these products. The photo is of the founder, and the letter is addressed to Elsie Booker, who owns this collection with her husband, John. The Booker Laboratories were in the family. *Courtesy of John & Elsie Booker, Patterson's Mill Country Store, Chapel Hill.*

Another mainstay of the drugstore was perfume and other personal care items. Armour reports that in his father's store the tobacco and perfume counters were opposite each other at the front of the store. "Men and women were thus separated before they had taken two steps into the store. If they came together again, it was at the counter in the rear where we displayed cold cures, which were of equal concern to both sexes."

The young Richard Armour was in charge of the perfume counter. He wrote:

"We sold perfume in bulk. On the shelves behind the counter were large, glass-stoppered bottles full of Rose, Violet, Lily of the Valley, Jasmine, Carnation, and various exotic and, the customers hoped, erotic mixtures. The way to sell perfume was to pull out stopper after stopper and wave it gently in front of the customer, who leaned over the counter within sniffing range. Once the customer decided on the scent and quantity, the perfume was poured into a graduated beaker and then into a small bottle or vial. This was taken back to the prescription room, where the name of the perfume was typed on a label which was pasted onto the bottle so the user would know what it was she was smelling of."[10]

The label of this Buffalo water bottle states all the healthful, healing qualities of the product. Lythia Springs Water Co., Lythia Springs, Virginia. *Courtesy of John & Elsie Booker, Patterson's Mill Country Store, Chapel Hill.*

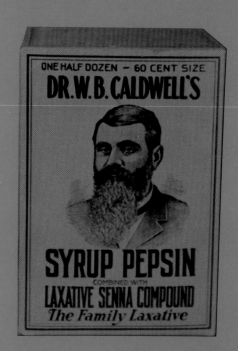

Paper Bromo-Seltzer advertisement, later glued to wood. Founded in Chapel Hill, North Carolina, Bromo-Seltzer was later prepared by the Emerson Drug Company, Baltimore, Maryland. 16″ x 12″. BK

Counter box for Dr. W.B. Caldwell's Syrup Pepsin. Cardboard, 7.75″ x 9.5″. *Courtesy of John & Elsie Booker, Patterson's Mill Country Store, Chapel Hill.*

BROMO-SELTZER FOR HEADACHES

Embossed tin Bromo-Seltzer sign. 9.25″ x 19.75″. *Courtesy of John & Elsie Booker, Patterson's Mill Country Store, Chapel Hill.*

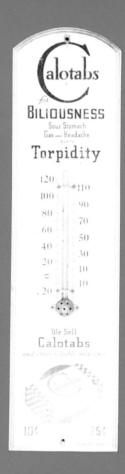

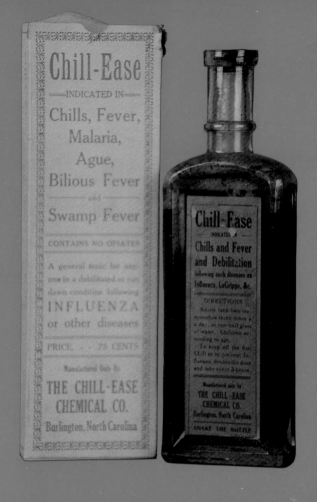

Wooden thermometer for Calotabs. 15″ x 4″. *Courtesy of John & Elsie Booker, Patterson's Mill Country Store, Chapel Hill.*

Chill-Ease bottle and box, The Chill-Ease Chemical Co., Burlington, North Carolina. *Courtesy of John & Elsie Booker, Patterson's Mill Country Store, Chapel Hill.*

Two boxes for Black Draught Pure Vegetable Laxative. The taller is 7″ x 3″. The shorter is 2.75″ x 1.5″. *Courtesy of John & Elsie Booker, Patterson's Mill Country Store, Chapel Hill.*

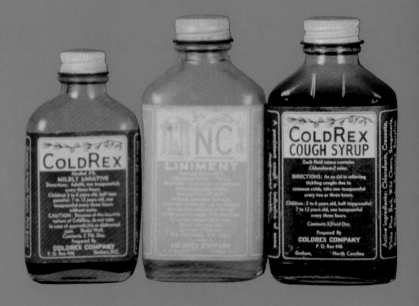

Three products of the Coldrex Company, Graham, North Carolina: A laxative, a liniment, and a cough syrup. *Courtesy of John & Elsie Booker, Patterson's Mill Country Store, Chapel Hill.*

87

A nice, reversed painted-on-glass electrified sign for Crazy Crystals. 7″ x 15.75″. *Courtesy of John & Elsie Booker, Patterson's Mill Country Store, Chapel Hill.*

Paper sign for Dr. A.C. Daniels' Cat and Dog Remedies. 18″ x 11″. *Courtesy of John & Elsie Booker, Patterson's Mill Country Store, Chapel Hill.*

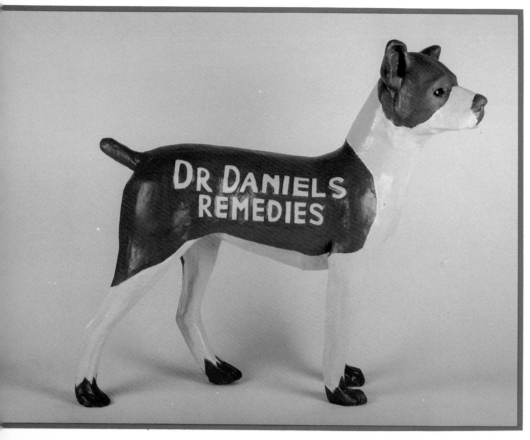

Dr. Daniels Dog advertisement. Composition with glass eyes, 23″ x 24″. *Courtesy of Koehler Bros. Inc.—The General Store, Lafayette, Indiana.*

This interesting paper poster gives a view of an old drug store featuring Dr. DeWitt's Household Remedies, c.1890. W.J. Parker & Co., Baltimore, Maryland. 21″ x 27″. *Courtesy of John & Elsie Booker, Patterson's Mill Country Store, Chapel Hill.*

Doan's Kidney Pills advertising thermometer. Wood, 21″ x 5.25″. *Courtesy of John & Elsie Booker, Patterson's Mill Country Store, Chapel Hill.*

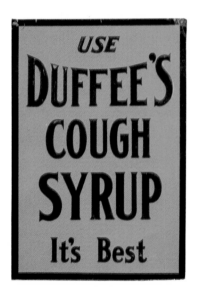

Oaken barrel for Dickinson's Witch Hazel. 10.5″ x 17.5″. *Courtesy of John & Elsie Booker, Patterson's Mill Country Store, Chapel Hill.*

Embossed tin sign for Duffee's Cough Syrup. 14″ x 9.5″. *Courtesy of John & Elsie Booker, Patterson's Mill Country Store, Chapel Hill.*

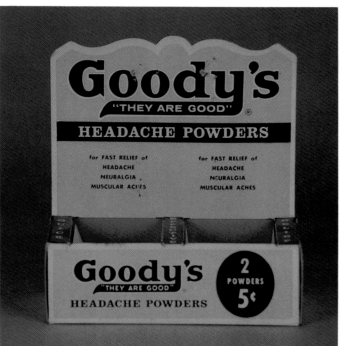

Advertising counter mirror for Gets-It Corn and Callous Remover, c. 1920s. 10.5″ x 8″. *Courtesy of Hook's Historic Drug Store & Pharmacy Museum, Indianapolis.*

Paper poster for Eskay's Baby Food, featuring Dorathea Jean Seltzer of Reading, Pennsylvania who was "raised exclusively on Eskay's food. 21.5″ x 13.5″. *Courtesy of John & Elsie Booker, Patterson's Mill Country Store, Chapel Hill.*

Tin container for Fleming's Colic Cure, Fleming Bros., Chemists, Chicago. *Courtesy of John & Elsie Booker, Patterson's Mill Country Store, Chapel Hill.*

Paper counter box for Goody's Headache Powders. 7″ x 6.5″ x 2.25″. *Courtesy of John & Elsie Booker, Patterson's Mill Country Store, Chapel Hill.*

Paper sign for Goody's Headache Powders. 18" x 19.5". *Courtesy of John & Elsie Booker, Patterson's Mill Country Store, Chapel Hill.*

Paper box for Grove's Cold Tablets, Grove Laboratories, St. Louis, Missouri. 1.5" x 7" 2.5". *Courtesy of John & Elsie Booker, Patterson's Mill Country Store, Chapel Hill.*

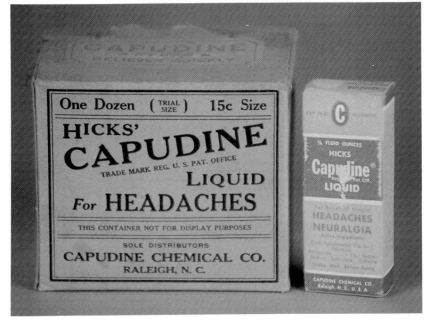

Box with sample size of Hick's Capudine Liquid for Headaches, Capudine Chemical Co., Raleigh, North Carolina. The large box is 3.25" x 4.5" x 3.75". *Courtesy of John & Elsie Booker, Patterson's Mill Country Store, Chapel Hill.*

Advertising puzzle for Hood's Sarsaparilla, c. 1890. The back has another puzzle in black and white. C.I. Hood & Co., Lowell, Massachusetts, 10″ x 14.5″. *Courtesy of Hook's Historic Drug Store & Pharmacy Museum, Indianapolis.*

Imported from France, the packaging and message of Hypotens Fraisse should have helped sales. It is called a Vaso-Motor Dilator and contains Sodium Nitrate & Extract of Mistletoe. *Courtesy of John & Elsie Booker, Patterson's Mill Country Store, Chapel Hill.*

A very nice Humphrey's Remedies cabinet. Oak and tin, it lists the Humphrey's homeopathic products by number, telling what they should be used to treat. *Courtesy of John & Elsie Booker, Patterson's Mill Country Store, Chapel Hill.*

A variety of the Humphrey Remedies and some of a similar product by Munyon.

A variety of the literature Humphrey's used to explain and promote its remedies. In the background is a wooden case used to carry the products. *Courtesy of John & Elsie Booker, Patterson's Mill Country Store, Chapel Hill.*

Illuminated reverse painted glass sign for Long Server cough syrup. 9.5" x 21". *Courtesy of John & Elsie Booker, Patterson's Mill Country Store, Chapel Hill.*

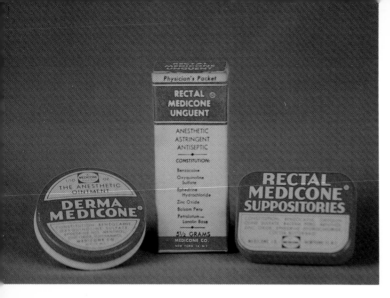

The Medicone Company of New York, New York, produced many salves, ointments, and suppositories. *Courtesy of John & Elsie Booker, Patterson's Mill Country Store, Chapel Hill.*

Mellin's Food milk modifier. *Courtesy of John & Elsie Booker, Patterson's Mill Country Store, Chapel Hill.*

1939 Miles calendar advertising their products, Alka-Seltzer and Dr. Miles Nervine, as well as Campbell's Drug Store in Maiden, North Carolina. 16″ x 10″. *Courtesy of John & Elsie Booker, Patterson's Mill Country Store, Chapel Hill.*

Sign for Minard's Liniment, circa 1940. *Courtesy of John & Elsie Booker, Patterson's Mill Country Store, Chapel Hill.*

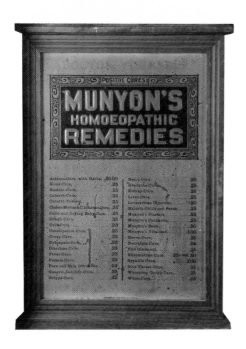

Nature's Remedy novelty advertising mirror. 2.5" in diameter. *Courtesy of Hook's Historic Drug Store & Pharmacy Museum, Indianapolis.*

Wood and tin cabinet for Munyon's Homeopathic Remedies, a competitor of Humphrey's. *Courtesy of John & Elsie Booker, Patterson's Mill Country Store, Chapel Hill.*

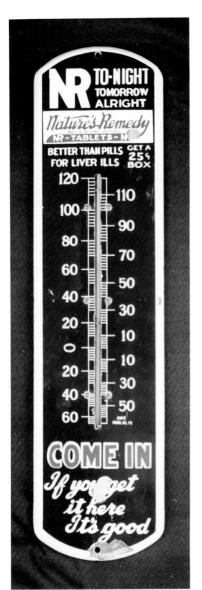

A paper fan from Clark's Pharmacy, Cillicothe, Missouri, advertising Nature's Remedy and Tums

Nature's Remedy enameled thermometer. 27" x 7". *Courtesy of John & Elsie Booker, Patterson's Mill Country Store, Chapel Hill.*

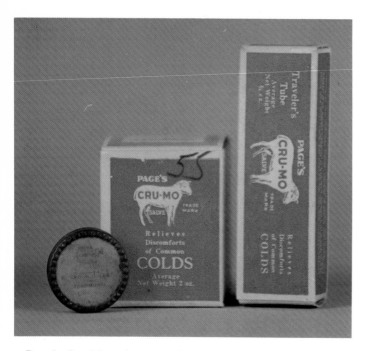

Page's Cru-Mo salves, used for the discomforts of colds. *Courtesy of John & Elsie Booker, Patterson's Mill Country Store, Chapel Hill.*

Die-cut self-standing cardboard Pepto-Bismal sign, with the bottles as separate stand-up pieces. Kindred, MacLean & Co., Inc., signed by the artist, Jerome Rozen. 41″ x 31″. *Courtesy of Koehler Bros. Inc.—The General Store, Lafayette, Indiana.*

The Peabody Drug Company of Durham, North Carolina, developed a number of products for national distribution. *Courtesy of John & Elsie Booker, Patterson's Mill Country Store, Chapel Hill.*

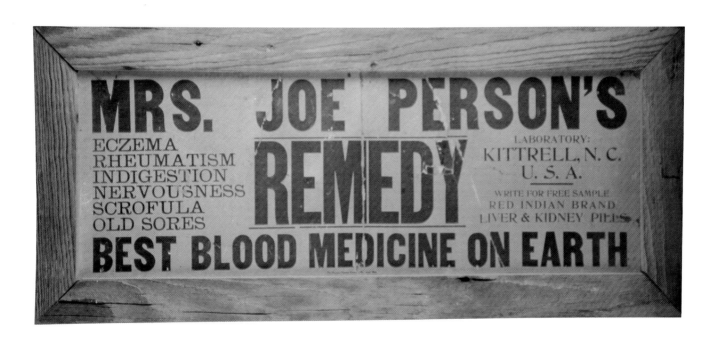

Paper sign for Mrs. Joe Person's Remedy, Kittrell, North Carolina. Kemper-Thomas, Cincinnati, Ohio, 9.75" x 28". *Courtesy of John & Elsie Booker, Patterson's Mill Country Store, Chapel Hill.*

Calendar advertising Lydia Pinkham's Vegetable Compound, 1926. 13" x 8". *Courtesy of John & Elsie Booker, Patterson's Mill Country Store, Chapel Hill.*

Paper advertisement for Dr. Pierce's Golden Medical Discovery, circa 1910. Niagara Litho Co., Buffalo, New York, 13.25" x 10.75". *Courtesy of John & Elsie Booker, Patterson's Mill Country Store, Chapel Hill.*

Dr. Pierce's Favorite Prescription paper poster, c. 1910. Niagara Litho Co., Buffalo, New York, 13.25″ x 10.75″. *Courtesy of John & Elsie Booker, Patterson's Mill Country Store, Chapel Hill.*

Two decals for Dr. Pierce products, c. 1915. Both exhibit the strong graphics that are typical of Dr. Pierce advertising, circa 1920. *Courtesy of John & Elsie Booker, Patterson's Mill Country Store, Chapel Hill.*

War time sign for Dr. Pierce's Medical Discovery, "A Bulwark of Strength." Circa 1917, 20″ x 16″. *Courtesy of John & Elsie Booker, Patterson's Mill Country Store, Chapel Hill.*

Three Dr. Pierce signs, c. 1915. Paper, 22″ long. *Courtesy of John & Elsie Booker, Patterson's Mill Country Store, Chapel Hill.*

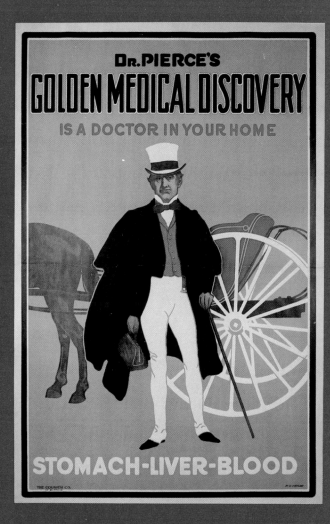

A beautiful paper poster for Dr. Pierce's Golden Medical Discovery, c. 1915. Printed by the Courier Co., of Buffalo. E.C. Pease, artist. 47" x 33". *Courtesy of John & Elsie Booker, Patterson's Mill Country Store, Chapel Hill.*

Two-part poster for Dr. Pierce's Anuric. Paper, 45" long c. 1915. *Courtesy of John & Elsie Booker, Patterson's Mill Country Store, Chapel Hill.*

Smaller cardboard sign for Dr. Pierce's Anuric. While it is not marked, it shows the strong graphic sense of E.C. Pease. Niagara Litho Co., Buffalo, New York. 13.25" x 10.75", c. 1915. *Courtesy of John & Elsie Booker, Patterson's Mill Country Store, Chapel Hill.*

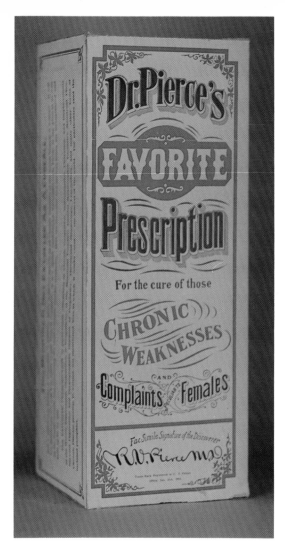

Cardboard display box for Dr. Pierce's Favorite Prescription. 19.5" x 8" x 8". *Courtesy of John & Elsie Booker, Patterson's Mill Country Store, Chapel Hill.*

Three war time signs showing how everyone must do their part, and, of course, that Dr. Pierce will too. Each is 42" long. *Courtesy of John & Elsie Booker, Patterson's Mill Country Store, Chapel Hill.*

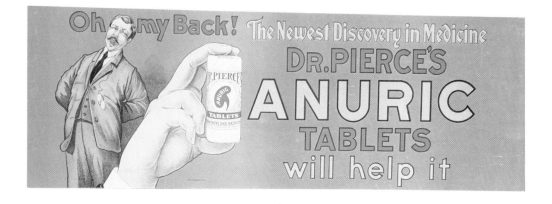

Paper poster for Dr. Pierce's Anuric tablets, c. 1915. 22" long. *Courtesy of John & Elsie Booker, Patterson's Mill Country Store, Chapel Hill.*

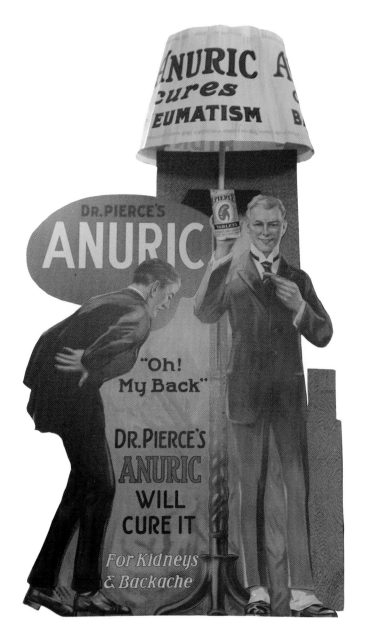

Lamp display for Dr. Pierce's Anuric. 22″ tall. *Courtesy of John & Elsie Booker, Patterson's Mill Country Store, Chapel Hill.*

Another Dr. Pierce sign notable for its strong graphics. Printed by the Courier Co., of Buffalo, c. 1915. E.C. Pease, artist. 47″ x 33″. *Courtesy of John & Elsie Booker, Patterson's Mill Country Store, Chapel Hill.*

Display box for Penetro Cough Drops, by St. Joseph's Laboratories, a division of Plough, Inc. 5″ x 4″ x 4″. *Courtesy of John & Elsie Booker, Patterson's Mill Country Store, Chapel Hill.*

101

A collection of Pratt animal products, often found sold at pharmacies as well as general stores. The rooster graphic on the left boxes is quite attractive. Pratt Food Company, Philadelphia, Pennsylvania. *Courtesy of John & Elsie Booker, Patterson's Mill Country Store, Chapel Hill.*

Two glass and tin containers for the smaller tin packages of Ramon's Brownie products. *Courtesy of John & Elsie Booker, Patterson's Mill Country Store, Chapel Hill.*

Thermometer for Ramon's Brownie Pills and Pink Pills. Tin, 21" x 9". *Courtesy of John & Elsie Booker, Patterson's Mill Country Store, Chapel Hill.*

Rice's salves, made by the Rice Chemical Company, Greensboro, New York. *Courtesy of John & Elsie Booker, Patterson's Mill Country Store, Chapel Hill.*

Calendar for the Sampson Medicine Company, 1939. Bamboo, 25.5" x 12". *Courtesy of John & Elsie Booker, Patterson's Mill Country Store, Chapel Hill.*

St. Jacobs Oil, "The Great German Remedy," was imported to U.S. drugstores. *Courtesy of John & Elsie Booker, Patterson's Mill Country Store, Chapel Hill.*

Products of the Scott Drug Co., Charlotte, North Carolina. Left to right: Nose drops; Nural-G-Lene treatment for headache and neuralgia; White Mustard Seed; and powder for preserving fruit. *Courtesy of John & Elsie Booker, Patterson's Mill Country Store, Chapel Hill.*

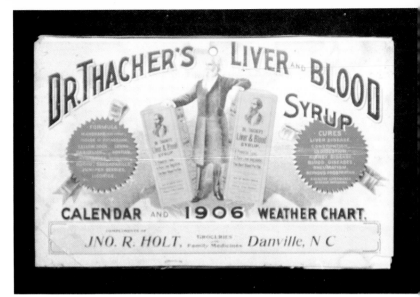

An advertising horse shoe for Simmon's Liver Regulator. 6.5″ x 5.5″. *Courtesy of John & Elsie Booker, Patterson's Mill Country Store, Chapel Hill.*

Nicely lithographed calendar and weather chart advertising Dr. Thacher's Liver and Blood Syrup. Calendars like this were produced by the patent medicine companies for distribution through drugstores to the consumers. This calendar was distributed by Jno. R. Holt, Danville, North Carolina. The calendar portion is missing. *Courtesy of John & Elsie Booker, Patterson's Mill Country Store, Chapel Hill.*

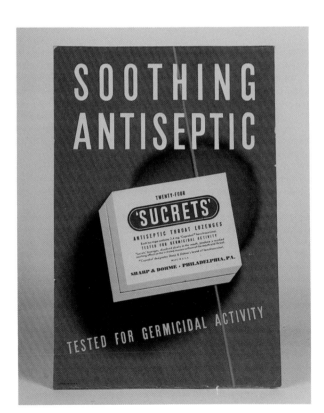

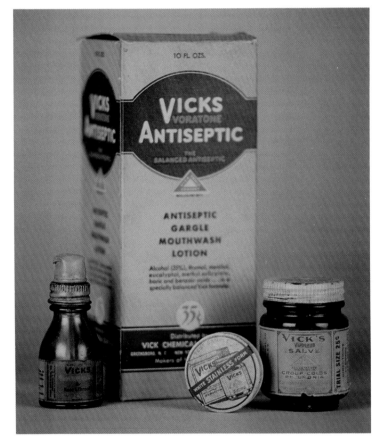

Self-standing cardboard Sucrets sign, 11″ x 8″. *Courtesy of John & Elsie Booker, Patterson's Mill Country Store, Chapel Hill.*

Vick's products originated at the Vick's Chemical Company in Greensboro, North Carolina, and grew into a national enterprise with offices in New York and Philadelphia. *Courtesy of John & Elsie Booker, Patterson's Mill Country Store, Chapel Hill.*

Beautiful lithographed die cut poster advertising Yager's Liniment. 21" x 28.5". *Courtesy of John & Elsie Booker, Patterson's Mill Country Store, Chapel Hill.*

Wyeth's Prepared Food bottle. Amber glass, 12.5" x 5" x 5". *Courtesy of John & Elsie Booker, Patterson's Mill Country Store, Chapel Hill.*

Assorted products of the Yerkes Chemical Company, Winston-Salem, North Carolina. *Courtesy of John & Elsie Booker, Patterson's Mill Country Store, Chapel Hill.*

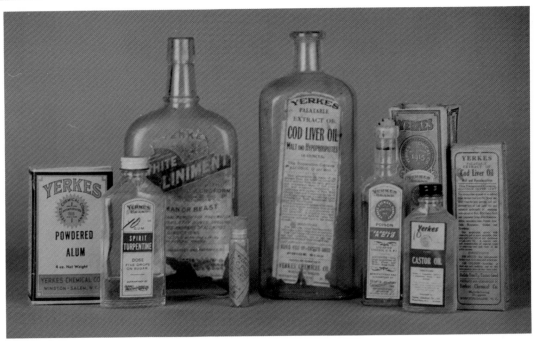

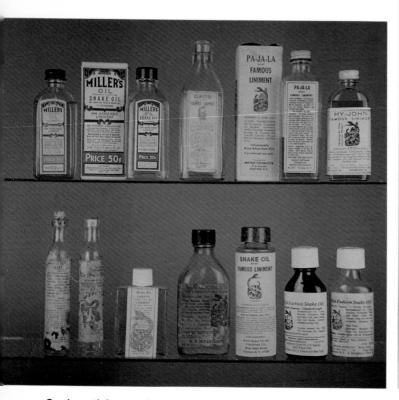

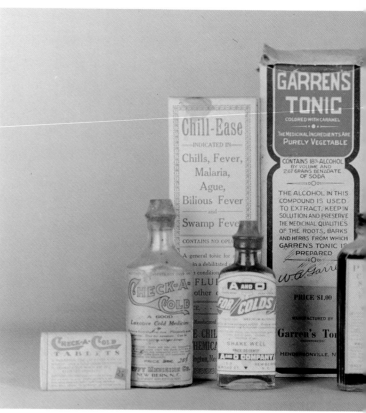

Snake oil brings back images of con men and carnies hawking their wares from the back of a wagon. "A cure for everything." For external use only, it purported to cure toothache, head and chest colds, corns, bunions, rheumatism, sore throats, and host of other ailments, by simply applying it to the affected part. *Courtesy of John & Elsie Booker, Patterson's Mill Country Store, Chapel Hill.*

Products of North Carolina drug companies. Left to right: Check-a-Cold, Duffy Medicine Co., New Bern; Chill-Ease, Chill-Ease Chemical, Burlington; A and O Company, New Bern; Garren's Tonic, Hendersonville; Pinee, Daly-Herring Co., Kinston; King Hero's Laxative, Eureka Dist. Co., Salemberg; Chex-It, Lumberton; Hall's Discovery, Atlas Chemical, Wilmington. *Courtesy of John & Elsie Booker, Patterson's Mill Country Store, Chapel Hill.*

Stand-up Rexall Drugstore Counter or Window display. Die-cut cardboard., 10" x 17". *Courtesy of Koehler Bros. Inc.— The General Store, Lafayette, Indiana.*

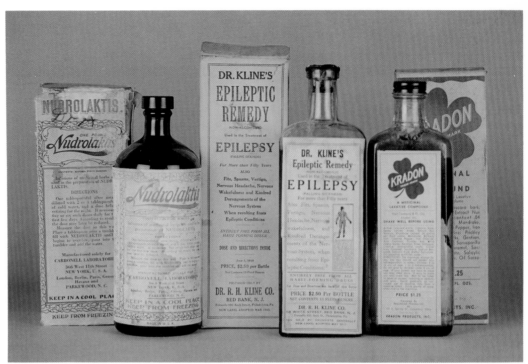

Boxes and bottles for: Neurolaktis, a tonic by Carbonell Laboratories, New York; Dr. Klines Epileptic Remedy, Dr. R.H. Kline Co., Red Bank, New Jersey; and Kradon laxative compound, Kradon Products, Inc., Columbus, Ohio. All 8-9.5 inches tall. *Courtesy of John & Elsie Booker, Patterson's Mill Country Store, Chapel Hill.*

Patent medicine boxes and bottles. Left to right: Maltine vitamin formula, Maltine Co., New York; Ner-Vigor compound for anemia, depression, and neurashthema, Huxley & Company, London; Phenol Sodique, an external antiseptic and cleaning agent, Hance Brothers and White, Philadelphia; Liv-O-Lax, a laxative by W.L. Hand Medicine Company, Charlotte, North Carolina. *Courtesy of John & Elsie Booker, Patterson's Mill Country Store, Chapel Hill.*

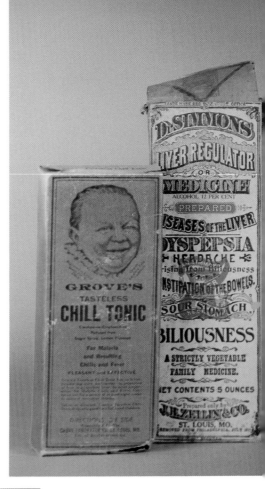

Assorted medicines. Left to right: Citrate of Magnesia, Miller's Goldboro Drug Co., Goldsboro, North Carolina; Phenophen laxative, Thigpen Distributing Co., Pikeville, North Carolina; Sals Ointment for Psoriasis, JLS Company, Plymouth, North Carolina; Oriole Brand North Carolina Pine Tar, James Corner & Sons, Baltimore, Maryland; Thomas' Indigestion Remedy, Mrs. Alberta Thomas, Wallburg, North Carolina. *Courtesy of John & Elsie Booker, Patterson's Mill Country Store, Chapel Hill.*

Left to right: Grove's Chill Tonic, Grove Laboratories, St. Louis; Dr. Simmon's Liver Regulator or Medicine, J.H. Zeilin & Company, St. Louis; Sanford's Cholera and Diarrhea Mixture, Gilbert Bros., & Co., Baltimore, Maryland; Celerina, Rio Chemical Co., New York. With 42% alcohol the Celerina should do a pretty fair job with "Functional Nervous Disorders"! *Courtesy of John & Elsie Booker, Patterson's Mill Country Store, Chapel Hill.*

Codamines vitamins, Frederick Stearns & Company, Detroit, Michigan; medicine bottle from Ch. S. Snead & Co., Lynchburg, Virginia; Gold Medal Vegetable Compound, S. Pfeiffer Mfg. Co., St. Louis, Missouri; Neurilla, Dad Chemical Co., New York; Kutnow's Powder, Kutnow Brothers, New York, Cos-Tal syrup of flaxseed licorice, wild cherry and menthol, Cos-Tal Laboratories, Savannah, Georgia. *Courtesy of John & Elsie Booker, Patterson's Mill Country Store, Chapel Hill.*

Left to right: Lithiated Hydrangea, Lambert, St. Louis; Dentasept, Chicago Pharmaceutical Co.; Alkalithia, Keasbey & Mattison, Ambler, Pennsylvania; Bishop's Varlettes Contrexeville Salts, Alfred Bishop, Ltd., London. *Courtesy of John & Elsie Booker, Patterson's Mill Country Store, Chapel Hill.*

Re-Cu-Ma, A Root and Herb Medicine, The National Remedy Co., Jacksonville, Florida; Lyko Tonic, Lyko Medicine Co., New York; Tryphonine, Reed and Carnick, Jersey City, New Jersey; Kola-Cardinette, Palisades Mfg., Yonkers, New York. *Courtesy of John & Elsie Booker, Patterson's Mill Country Store, Chapel Hill.*

Patent medicines. Left to right: Nutritive, Henry Thayer &
Co., Cambridgeport, Massachusetts; Swindell's 999 iron
tonic, Swindell's Health & Beauty Products, Baltimore;
BBB, Standard Laboratories, New York & St. Louis.
*Courtesy of John & Elsie Booker, Patterson's Mill Country
Store, Chapel Hill.*

Patent medicines. Left to right:
Sumlakia, a non-alcoholic, non-
narcotic sedative, the Sumlak
Company, Cincinnati; Athen-
staedt Tincture of Iron, Lehn &
Fink, New York; Williams
Formula, a mild laxative,
Milwaukee; Yager's Compound
Extract Sarsaparilla with
Celery, Gilbert Bros., & Co.,
Baltimore, Maryland. *Courtesy
of John & Elsie Booker, Patter-
son's Mill Country Store,
Chapel Hill.*

Patent medicines. Left to right: Cascara-Peptonoids (Tonic
Laxative), Arlington Chemical, Yonkers, New York; Epson
Salts, First National Pharmacy, Lehighton, Pennsylvania;
Hicks Capudine Liquid for headaches and neuralgia,
Caudine Chemical Co., Raleigh, North Carolina; Booker's
Cough Remedy, Booker Laboratories, Norfolk, Virginia.
*Courtesy of John & Elsie Booker, Patterson's Mill Country
Store, Chapel Hill.*

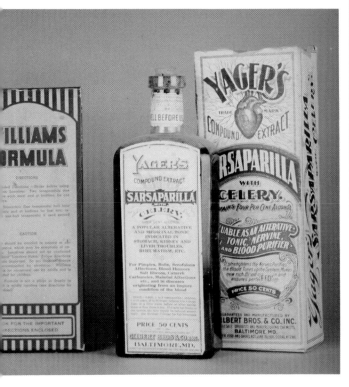

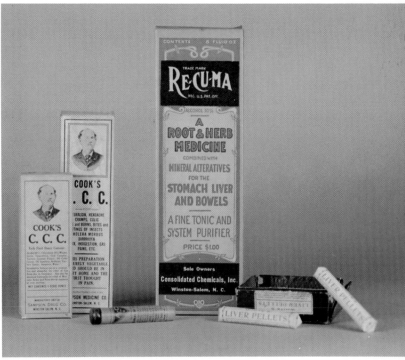

Patent medicines. Left to right: Cook's C.C.C., a cure-all from the Sampson Drug Co., Winston-Salem, North Carolina; A.C. tablets, A.C. Co., Raleigh, North Carolina; Re-Cu-Ma, A Root & Herb Medicine, Consolidated Chemicals, Inc., Winston-Salem, North Carolina; White's Liver Pellets, Mebane Drug Co., Mebane, North Carolina. *Courtesy of John & Elsie Booker, Patterson's Mill Country Store, Chapel Hill.*

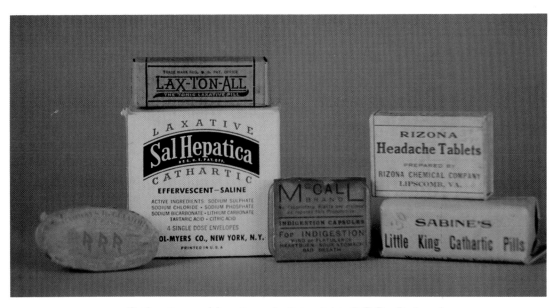

Cathartics and laxatives. Left to right: R.R.R., Radway's Regulators, New York; Lax-Ton-All, New York; Sal Hepatica, Bristol Myers, New York; McCall Indigestion Capsules; Rizona Headache Tablets, Rizona Chemical Company, Lipscomb, Virginia; Sabines Little King Cathartic Pills, A.J. Lemke, Milwaukee. *Courtesy of John & Elsie Booker, Patterson's Mill Country Store, Chapel Hill.*

111

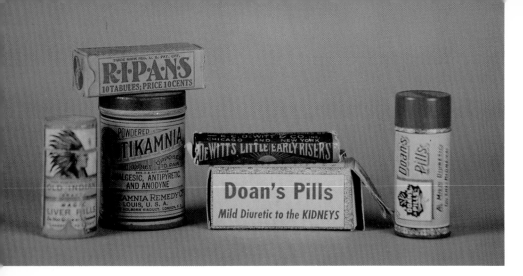

Patented remedies. Left to right: nicely lithographed Old Indian liver pill tube, paper on cardboard; Ripans, Wyeth, Detroit; Antikamnia Analgesic tin, 2.5"; DeWitt's Little Early Risers Cathartic, E.C. DeWitt & Co., Chicago, 2.75"; Doan's Pills tin, 2.75". *Courtesy of John & Elsie Booker, Patterson's Mill Country Store, Chapel Hill.*

Remedies: Left to right: Dr. Morse's Indian Root, W.H. Comstock Co., Morristown, New Jersey, 2.75"; Lyman Brown's Compound, New York, 3.5"; a later package of Dr. Morse's Indian Root; B. Brandreth's V. V. Pills, 2.75"; Gum Assafoetida, Murray Drug, Columbia, South Carolina; Cole's Blood & Liver Pills, Durham, North Carolina, glass; Pape's "Cold" Compound, Sterling Products, Wheeling, West Virginia. *Courtesy of John & Elsie Booker, Patterson's Mill Country Store, Chapel Hill.*

Remedies. Left to right: Mothersill's Airsick Remedy, Ferd. T. Hopkins & Sons, New York, 2.25" x 1.5"; ExLax Sample, Brooklyn, New York, 1.75" x 1.75"; Cascarets counter box, 1.5" x 4" x 3.25", and tin 1.5" x 2", R.L. Walkin Co., New York. *Courtesy of John & Elsie Booker, Patterson's Mill Country Store, Chapel Hill.*

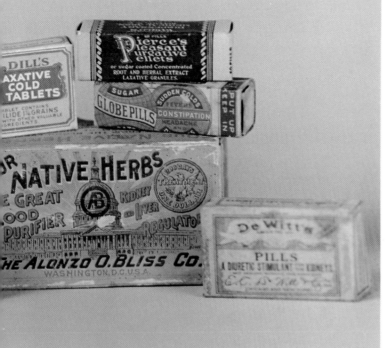

Patented pills. Left to right: Booth's Mi-O-Na tablets, Ithaca, New York, 3.25″; Dill's Laxative Cold Tablets, Norristown, Pennsylvania, 2.25″; OUr Native Herbs, The Great Blood Purifier, The Alonzo O. Bliss Company, Washington, D.C., 2.75″ x 5″; Dr. Pierce's Pleasant Purgative Pellets, 3″; Globe Pills, New York, 3″; DeWitt's Pills, A Diuretic Stimulant for the Kidneys, E.C. DeWitt & Co., Chicago, 3″. *Courtesy of John & Elsie Booker, Patterson's Mill Country Store, Chapel Hill.*

1912 Almanac advertising Dr. Morse's Indian Root Pills. Paper, 34 pages, 6″ x 6.25″. *Courtesy of Hook's Historic Drug Store & Pharmacy Museum, Indianapolis.*

A cardboard self-standing sign for Dr. Morse's Indian Root Pills. 9.5″ x 20″. *Courtesy of John & Elsie Booker, Patterson's Mill Country Store, Chapel Hill.*

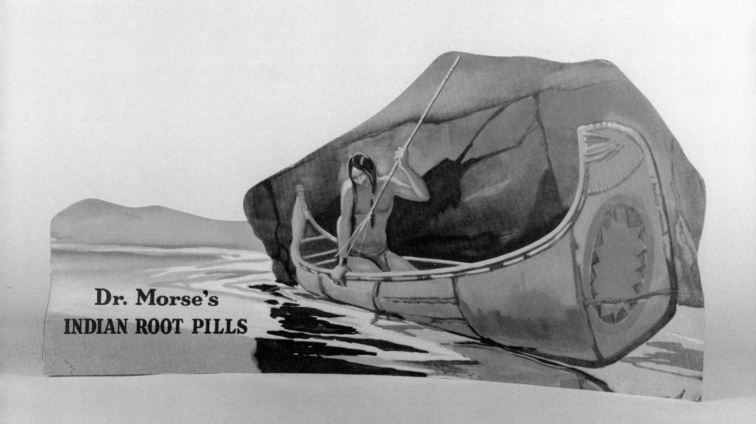

Lithia water bottles. Left: Lincoln Lithia, Lithia Springs, Virginia. Right: Buffalo Lithia Water. A cure for almost everything, the usual dose of Lithia water was 6-8 glasses per day. *Courtesy of John & Elsie Booker, Patterson's Mill Country Store, Chapel Hill.*

Veterinary powders. Left: Dr. David Roberts' Soothing Paste for coughs in livestock, Dr. David Roberts Veterinary Co., Waukesha, Wisconsin. Tin with paper label, 6″ x 4″. Right: Dr. A.C. Daniel's Poultry Louse Powder, Dr. A.C. Daniels, Inc., Boston. Cardboard cylinder with tin ends and paper label, 6.5″ x 3″. *Courtesy of John & Elsie Booker, Patterson's Mill Country Store, Chapel Hill.*

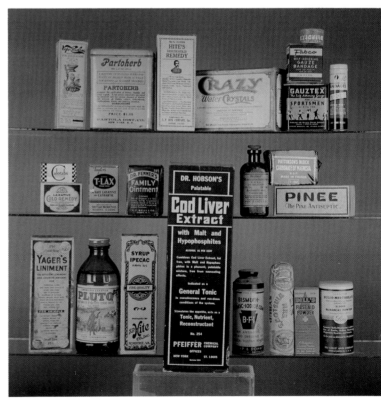

The message is clear on these bottles. Both the bottles and the pills within are shaped like coffins. The pills are marked "Poison," and contain Mercuric chloride. Cobalt glass with paper label (name illegible), 8″ x 3.5″. *Courtesy of Hook's Historic Drug Store & Pharmacy Museum, Indianapolis.*

Powders, soaps, and ointments. Left to right: Mentholatum sample, 3.5" x 2.5"; Columbia Powder sample, F.C. Sturtevant Co., Hartford, Connecticut, 1.5"; Unguentine, Norwich Pharmaceutical Co., Norwich, New York, 3.25"; El Estado Lemon Creme, 4.25"; Packer's Pine Tar Soap, Packer Co., Mystic, Connecticut; Wernet's Powder, 2.25". *Courtesy of John & Elsie Booker, Patterson's Mill Country Store, Chapel Hill.*

Opposite page bottom right:

Top shelf: Vapo-Cresolene for inhalation, Vapo-Cresolene, New York; Partoherb tin, Partola Dist. Co., New York; Hite's Remedy, S.P. Hite Co., Roanoke, Virginia; Crazy Water Crystals; Wet-Pruf tape; Fabco Gauze Bandage; Gauztex bandage, General Bandages, Chicago; tin for sterilized bandages. Middle shelf: Calotabs container; Ads Laxative Cold Remedy, American Druggists Syndicate, New York; Taylor's T-Lax, T-Lax Products, Bessemer, Alabama; Dr. Fenner's Family Ointment, S.C. Wells, & Co., Leroy, New York; cobalt blue bottle for Puretest Mercurochrome, United Drug Co., Boston; Pattinson's Block Carbonate of Magnesia; Pinee, The Pine Antiseptic. Bottom shelf: Yager's Liniment, Pluto Spring Water bottle; Syrup Ipecac, S.P. Hite, Roanoke, Virginia; Dr. Hobson's Cod Liver Extract; Pfeiffer Chemical Company, New York; Bismuth Formic-Iodide Compound, Sharp & Dohme, Philadelphia; Mrs. Winslow's Syrup; Dill's First Aid Powder, The Dill Company, Norristown, Pennsylvania; Sulfo-Merthiolate, Eli Lilly, Indianapolis, Indiana. *Courtesy of John & Elsie Booker, Patterson's Mill Country Store, Chapel Hill.*

Top shelf: Rawleigh Cathartic Pills, Antiseptic Salve, and Medicated Ointment, W.T. Rawleigh Company, Freeport; Vaseline Camphor Ice; Skeeto-Go bug repellent; Rawleigh Mustard Compound; Cocoa Butter. Middle shelf: Menthol Camphor Ointment,. Laxative Cold Tablets, and Vitamins A & D, J.R. Watkins Co., Newark, New Jersey; Liv-O-Med, Pure Drug Products; Daddy's Salve. Bottom shelf: Watkins Liniment and Petro-Carbo Salve; Florida Water; Rawleigh's Antiseptic Foot Powder; Tonic Tablets, Ho-Ro-Co, Mfg. Co., St. Louis, Missouri; Scabenzate Lotion, Hart Drug Corporation, Miami, Florida; The Genuine Indian Blood Purifier, Pearson Remedy Co., Burlington, North Carolina. *Courtesy of John & Elsie Booker, Patterson's Mill Country Store, Chapel Hill.*

Top shelf: Borated Tar Soap, Larkin Soap Co., Buffalo, New York; Milk of Magnesia Cold Cream Soap; Qban Toilet and Shampoo Soap, The Hessic Ellis Drug Co., Memphis. Middle shelf: Phenol Sodique Soap, Hance Brothers and White, Philadelphia; Cuticura Soap; Pears Transparent Soap. Bottom soap: Grand Union No-dope Cough Syrup; Larkin Cough Syrup, Larkin Co., Buffalo, New York; Shiloh for Coughs, S.C. Wells & Co., Leroy, New York; Mohawk's Pioneer Cough Remedy, Mohawk Remedy Co., Columbus, Ohio; Baseball Liniment, the bottle and new and old packaging. The bottle and left box are marked Hege Laboratories, Lexington, North Carolina, while the other box is marked Pearson's Remedy Co., Burlington, North Carolina. *Courtesy of John & Elsie Booker, Patterson's Mill Country Store, Chapel Hill.*

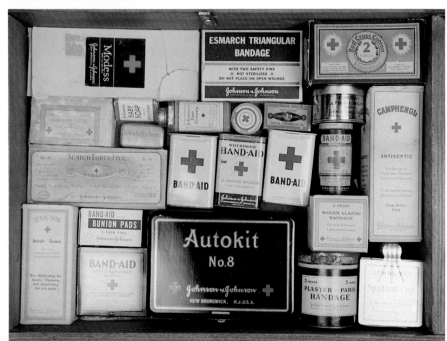

Assorted first aid supplies.

Advertising novelties from various drug companies. Left to right: Pierce's Memorandum and Account Book; Lydia Pinkham sewing kit; Ginger Mint Julep matches; pharmacy coasters; Coricidin playing cards; Bromo Seltzer memo book; die cut Bromo Seltzer pin folder; Johnson & Johnson *Handbook of First Aid.*

Cobalt blue glass bottles for Bromo-Seltzer, Emerson Drug Co., Baltimore, Maryland. 3"—8". *Courtesy of John & Elsie Booker, Patterson's Mill Country Store, Chapel Hill.*

Left to right: Mellins Infant Food, Boston, Massachusetts; Maine Condensed Milk Company; Harlich's Malted Milk, Racine, Wisconsin. *Courtesy of John & Elsie Booker, Patterson's Mill Country Store, Chapel Hill.*

Cobalt blue glass bottles. Left to right: Squibb's Milk of Magnesia (2); Charles H. Phillips Milk of Magnesia, Glenbrook, Connecticut; Hart Drug Co.; Wyeth Laboratories; Sodium Phosphate bottle with measuring cap, John Wyeth & Brother, Philadelphia. *Courtesy of John & Elsie Booker, Patterson's Mill Country Store, Chapel Hill.*

Left to right: Charles Dennis' Certain Cure for Rheumatism; Phillips Milk of Magnesia; R.R.R., Radway & Co., New York; Blancard; Dr. Harter's Wild Cherry Bitters. 6.5"—8". *Courtesy of John & Elsie Booker, Patterson's Mill Country Store, Chapel Hill.*

Left to right: Citrate of Magnesia; Citrated Magnesia; Syrup of Hypophosphates; (amber bottles) Kepler Malt, Burrows-Wellcome Co.; unknown; Peptonoids, Arlington Chemical Co. 6.75"—8". *Courtesy of John & Elsie Booker, Patterson's Mill Country Store, Chapel Hill.*

Bottles showing the variation that could occur over the life of a product. Left to right: The Piso Company, Hazeltine & Co. (3); Sloan's N&B Liniment, Sloan's Liniment Kills Pain, and Sloan's Liniment, Dr. E.S. Sloan, Boston. 5.5". *Courtesy of John & Elsie Booker, Patterson's Mill Country Store, Chapel Hill.*

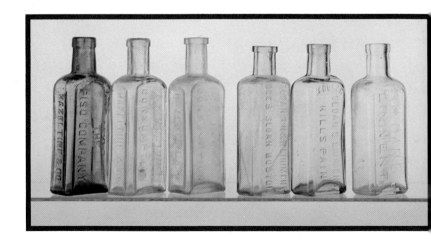

Left to right: Chamberlain's Cholic-Cholera Remedy; Spark's Perfect Health for Kidney and Liver Diseases; Florida Water, Murray & Lanman Druggists, New York; Roche's Embrocition for the Whooping Cough; Dr. Hayne's Arabian Balsam, E. Morgan & Sons, Providence, Rhode Island; Dr. J.W. Bull's Cough Syrup, Baltimore, Maryland; Dotson's Liver Tone. 4"—7.5". *Courtesy of John & Elsie Booker, Patterson's Mill Country Store, Chapel Hill.*

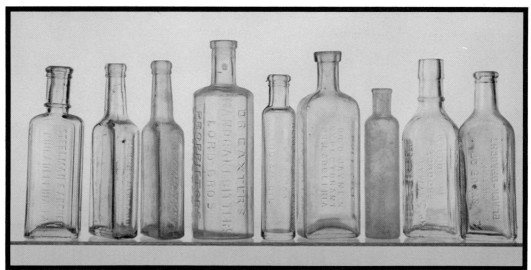

Left to right: Steelman & Archer, Philadelphia; Dr. Fletcher's Castoria, clear and frosted; Dr. Baxter's Mandrake Bitters, Lord Brothers,Proprietors, Burlington, Vermont; Healey & Bigelow Kickapoo Indian Oil; Dr. D. Jayne's Expectorant, Philadelphia; Unknown; Dr. T. Sayman, St. Louis; Thedford's Syrup of Black Draught. 5"—6.5". *Courtesy of John & Elsie Booker, Patterson's Mill Country Store, Chapel Hill.*

Left to right: St. Joseph's; Buck's Cholera, Dysentery, Diarrhea Cordial, Chelsea, Massachusetts; Kendall's Cure; Certisidin Porpoicidin, Philadelphia; Hall's Catarrh Cure; Doc Marshall's Catarrh Snuff; Dr. Kilmer's Swamp Root Kidney Cure; Re Umberto. 3.25"—6". *Courtesy of John & Elsie Booker, Patterson's Mill Country Store, Chapel Hill.*

Left to right: Omega Oil, "It's Green," Omega Chemical Co., New York; Tonsiline for Sore Throats; Dr. S.A. Tuttle, Boston; H.H. Hay & Sons, Portland, Maine; Dr. Caldwell's Laxative Sienna; Chamberlain's Pain Balm; Dr. Boscher's German Syrup. 5"—7". *Courtesy of John & Elsie Booker, Patterson's Mill Country Store, Chapel Hill.*

Davis Vegetable Pain Killer; McCormick & Co., Bee-brand, Baltimore; Cheeseman's Arabian Balsam; Monell's Teething Cordial; H. Clay Clover Co., New York; Predigestive Food Co., Paskola; Atlas Medicine Company, Henderson, North Carolina. 4.5"—6.25". *Courtesy of John & Elsie Booker, Patterson's Mill Country Store, Chapel Hill.*

Left to right: Hood's Sarsaparilla (2); Moxie; Moxie Nerve Food. 9"-11". *Courtesy of John & Elsie Booker, Patterson's Mill Country Store, Chapel Hill.*

Left to right: Milk's Emulsion; Essence of Pepsin, Fairchild Bros., & Foster, New York; fish-shaped bottle; Dr. Cumming's Vegetine. *Courtesy of John & Elsie Booker, Patterson's Mill Country Store, Chapel Hill.*

Left to right: Dr. Pierce's Golden Medical Discovery; Dr. Pierce's Favorite Prescription; Healey & Bigelow Indian Sagwa; Dr. Green's Nervura. 9". *Courtesy of John & Elsie Booker, Patterson's Mill Country Store, Chapel Hill.*

Dr. Mile's products (left to right): Dr. Miles Medical Co.; New Heart Cure; Nervine; Restorative Nervine. 8.5" tall. *Courtesy of John & Elsie Booker, Patterson's Mill Country Store, Chapel Hill.*

Left to right: Rawleigh's bottles (2); Warner's Safe Kidney & Liver Cure, West Chester, New York; Winstead's Lax-Fos; W.F. Kidder, New York. 7"—9.25". *Courtesy of John & Elsie Booker, Patterson's Mill Country Store, Chapel Hill.*

Left to right: Lydia Pinkham's Vegetable Compound; Creomulsion for Coughs due to Colds; Scott's Emulsion; Scott's Emulsion, Cod Liver Oil with Lime and Soda; Dr. Sanford's

Left to right: Dr. Kilmer's Swamp Root, Kidney, Liver, and Bladder Cure, Binghamton, New York; Dr. King's New Discovery for coughs and colds; California Fig Syrup Co., San Francisco; Wilbur's Javex; Dr. Peter Fahrney & Sons Co., Chicago, Illinois; Var-Ne-Sis. 10" tall. *Courtesy of John & Elsie Booker, Patterson's Mill Country Store, Chapel Hill.*

Left to right: Father John's Medicine, Lowell, Massachusetts; Hankin's Specific, Bordentown, New Jersey; The Mother's Friend, Atlanta, Georgia; Sarsaparilla, Lowell, Massachusetts; Dr. Kilmer's Swamp Root, Kilmer's

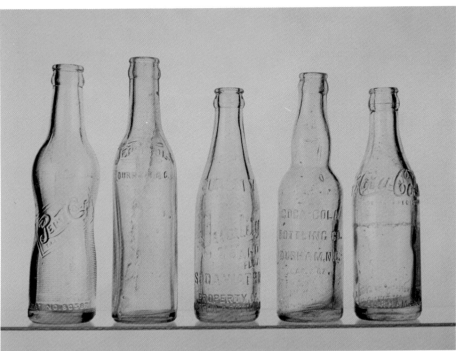

Liver Invigorator, New York; Astor, Puritan Drug Co., Columbus, Ohio. 8″—9.25″. *Courtesy of John & Elsie Booker, Patterson's Mill Country Store, Chapel Hill.*

Soda bottles (left to right): Pepsi-Cola; Pepsi-Cola, Durham, North Carolina; Quality brand soda water; Coca-Cola, Durham; Coca-Cola. 7.75″—8.5″. *Courtesy of John & Elsie Booker, Patterson's Mill Country Store, Chapel Hill.*

Medical Co., Cincinnati, Ohio; Dr. Guertun's Nerve Syrup. 7″—9.75″. *Courtesy of John & Elsie Booker, Patterson's Mill Country Store, Chapel Hill.*

Left to right: Minion's Paw-Paw; Lash's Bitters; Binz's Bronc-O-Lyptus for Coughs; Dr. Kennedy's Favorite Remedy; Dr. Kennedy's Medical Discovery; Veronica's Medical Spring Water. 8.5″—10.75″. *Courtesy of John & Elsie Booker, Patterson's Mill Country Store, Chapel Hill.*

Soda bottles (left to right): Christo Cola, Durham, North Carolina (2); Carolina Soda Water Co., Durham; Carolina Bottling Works, Durham; Mint Cola Bottling Co. 7.5"—9". *Courtesy of John & Elsie Booker, Patterson's Mill Country Store, Chapel Hill.*

Four Roses 100 Proof. During prohibition alcohol was sold through drugstores for its "medicinal" effects. This is advertised as "An alcoholic stimulant made from the fermented mash of grain." Satirical cartoons of the time were filled with images of the druggist as bartender, so it is doubtful that the euphemisms fooled anyone. *Courtesy of Hook's Historic Drug Store & Pharmacy Museum, Indianapolis.*

Three alcohol bottles (left to right): Indianapolis Brewing; Anheuser-Busch Brewing Association, St. Louis; The Duffy Malt Whiskey Co., Rochester, New York. *Courtesy of Hook's Historic Drug Store & Pharmacy Museum, Indianapolis.*

HOME CARE PRODUCTS

Left: Merrill's Suppository Machine, stainless steel, 3.5″ long. B & K Suppository Machine, Milwaukee, Wisconsin. *Courtesy of John & Elsie Booker, Patterson's Mill Country Store, Chapel Hill.*

A barrel of crutches. *Courtesy of John & Elsie Booker, Patterson's Mill Country Store, Chapel Hill.*

As an advertising promotion Kuftat drugs made replica of antique inhalers, which themselves are now collectible. This is a Double Maw's Valved Earthenware Inhaler, originally manufactured by S. Maw Son and Thompson, London. *Courtesy of John & Elsie Booker, Patterson's Mill Country Store, Chapel Hill.*

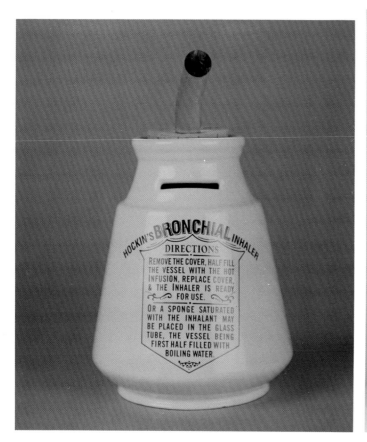

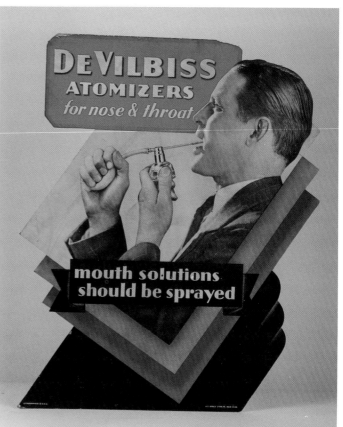

A reproduction of the Hockins Bronchial Inhaler. *Courtesy of John & Elsie Booker, Patterson's Mill Country Store, Chapel Hill.*

Cardboard counter advertisement for DeVilbiss Atomizers. A.C. Schulz Litho. Co., Milwaukee and Chicago. 21" x 17". *Courtesy of Koehler Bros. Inc.—The General Store, Lafayette, Indiana.*

Mystic Steam Atomizer, Whitall, Tatum & Co., New York. The steam created in the boiler would mix with the medication from the square reservoir and be inhaled through the face shield. *Courtesy of Hook's Historic Drug Store & Pharmacy Museum, Indianapolis.*

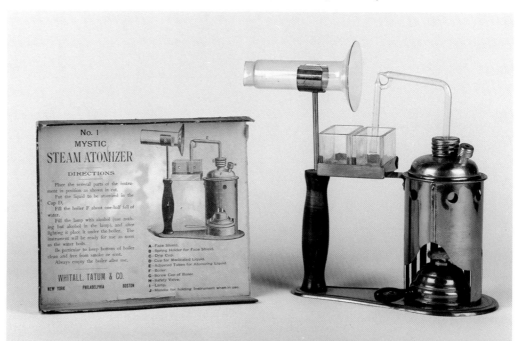

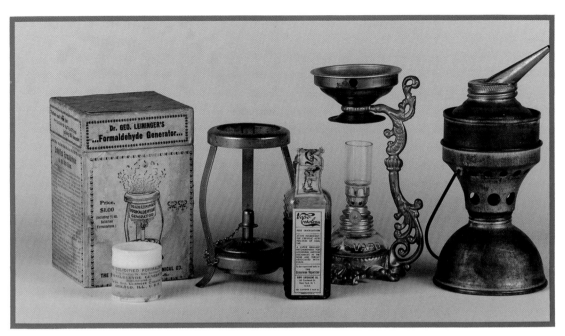

Various vaporizers. Left: Dr. George Leininger's
Formaldehyde Generator used for disinfecting a sickroom,
Chicago, Illinois. Shown with original box and medication
jar. Middle: Vapo-Cresolene Vapor Inhalant, shown with
medication. Vapo-Cresolene, New York. Atlas steam
vaporizer, No. 111. All are about 6″ high. *Courtesy of
Hook's Historic Drug Store & Pharmacy Museum,
Indianapolis.*

Atomizers (left to right): Glass atomizer with amber globe
and rubber pump, c. 1900. Sunburst alcohol burner; Turpo
Electric Vaporizer, glass and metal, shown with its original
box. Glessner Co., Findlay, Ohio. Electric Steam Vaporizer,
the DeVilbiss Company, Toledo, Ohio. Aluminum. *Courtesy
of Hook's Historic Drug Store & Pharmacy Museum,
Indianapolis.*

An aluminum DeVilbiss No. 146 Vaporizer. 7″ x 6″. *Courtesy of John & Elsie Booker, Patterson's Mill Country Store, Chapel Hill.*

Another Bauer & Black counter box, this one is for medicated plasters. 6.5″ x 8.5″ x 13.75″ with three drawers. *Courtesy of John & Elsie Booker, Patterson's Mill Country Store, Chapel Hill.*

Cardboard counter box for Bauer & Black Zinc Oxide Adhesive Plasters. 7.5″ x 7″ x 7″ with three drawers. *Courtesy of John & Elsie Booker, Patterson's Mill Country Store, Chapel Hill.*

Wooden Bauer & Black Corn and Bunion Plasters counter box. 11″ x 11″ x 8″. *Courtesy of John & Elsie Booker, Patterson's Mill Country Store, Chapel Hill.*

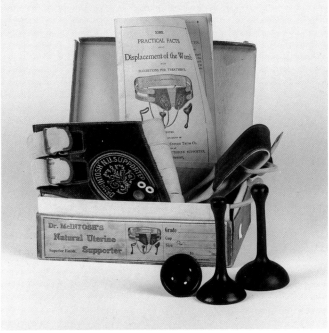

Early Bauer & Black counter box. Six drawers, cardboard 13.5″ x 13″ x 8″. *Courtesy of John & Elsie Booker, Patterson's Mill Country Store, Chapel Hill.*

Dr. McIntosh's Natural Uterine Supporter, for "displacement of the womb." This contraption of cloth, leather, and plastic was designed to right things that had gone wrong. *Courtesy of Hook's Historic Drug Store & Pharmacy Museum, Indianapolis.*

Seabury's Sanitary Pocket Cuspidor, Seabury & Johnson, New York. This accordion folded heavy paper envelope was filled with absorbent cotton, which would hold about 24 hours worth of "normal" spitting. *Courtesy of John & Elsie Booker, Patterson's Mill Country Store, Chapel Hill.*

Assorted syringe equipment and a hot water bag. *Courtesy of John & Elsie Booker, Patterson's Mill Country Store, Chapel Hill.*

PERSONAL CARE PRODUCTS

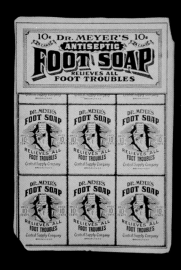

A three dimensional counter or window display for products of the Colgate-Palmolive Co. features delightful images of the drugstore, its products and customers. Circa 1920s. Cardboard, 31″ x 40″ x 20″. *Courtesy of Koehler Bros. Inc.—The General Store, Lafayette, Indiana.*

Advertisement for Dr. Myer's Antiseptic Foot Soap. Central Supply Company, Brooklyn, New York. Paper, 10″ x 7″. *Courtesy of John & Elsie Booker, Patterson's Mill Country Store, Chapel Hill.*

Die-cut advertisement for Elastic Starch with four beautiful children. Cardboard, 13″ x 19″. *Courtesy of Hook's Historic Drug Store & Pharmacy Museum, Indianapolis.*

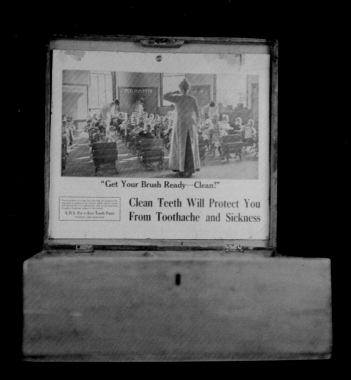

Counter box and changeable poster for Peredixo Tooth Paste. 6″ H x 14″ W x 12.5″ D. *Courtesy of John & Elsie Booker, Patterson's Mill Country Store, Chapel Hill.*

Die-cut advertisement for Bickmore Easy-Shave Cream. 30.5″ tall. *Courtesy of John & Elsie Booker, Patterson's Mill Country Store, Chapel Hill.*

The Peredixo family was created to advertise A.D.S. (American Druggists Syndicate, New York) Peredixo Tooth Paste. Given as premiums, they could be made to stand up by folding the "wings" of the base back. Each have the Peredixo tube printed on the back (top center). They are paper with the large tube measuring 20″ and the others 6.5″. *Courtesy of John & Elsie Booker, Patterson's Mill Country Store, Chapel Hill.*

Assorted soaps, creams, powders, and salves. Top (l-r): Golden Peacock Soap box, Paris Toilet Co., Paris, Tennessee; Soap box, copyright 1920, The Sterling Pin Co.; Rexall Disappearing Skin Cream, United Drug Co., Boston; Sopronol Powder, Mycoloid Laboratories, Little Falls, New Jersey; embossed aluminum cap of Larkin Cold Cream jar, Larkin Chemical, Buffalo; Cloverine Salve, Lambda Pharmacal Laboratories, New York. Middle (l-r): Perfect Complexion Powder, Tetlow Mfg. Co.; Dabrook's Face Powder, New York; unknown; Black & White Face Powder, Plough, Inc., New York; Mellier's Oriana Face Powder, Mellier, New York. Bottom (l-r): Violet Dulce Cold Cream, Harmony of Boston; Miner's American Rice Face Powder, Henry C. Miner, New York; Bermarine Face Powder tin; Tetley Pussywillow Powder; Dilnorpa Face Powder. *Courtesy of John & Elsie Booker, Patterson's Mill Country Store, Chapel Hill.*

Soaps, powders, and lotions. Top (l-r): Mercirex Medicated Soap; Stieffel's Ichthammol Soap; Grandpa's Wonder Pine Tar Toilet Soap, Latner's; Physicians & Surgeons Soap; Cary Lee Witch Hazel; Lusier's Powder. Middle (l-r): DeLoney's Medicated Soap, DeLoney & Co., Chicago; Poslam Soap; White's Specific Soap; Bermarine Shampoo and Skin Soap; Tellerine Soap; Resinol Toilet and Bath Soap. Bottom (l-r): Quitch toilet powder, New York; Dr. Sayman's Toilet Powder; Ammen's Brickly Heat Baby Powder, Charles Ammen Co. Chemists, Alexandria, Virginia; Allen's Foot Ease, United Sales & Mfg. Co., Buffalo; Gill's Foot Soap, Thomas Gill Soap Co., Brooklyn; Azomis Toilet and Nursery Powder, Sharp & Dohme, Baltimore; Meritt Powder; Amolin Deodorant Powder, Norwich Chemical Co. *Courtesy of John & Elsie Booker, Patterson's Mill Country Store, Chapel Hill.*

Various opal glass cold cream jars with embossed tops. *Courtesy of John & Elsie Booker, Patterson's Mill Country Store, Chapel Hill.*

Ointments, scents, and powders. Top (l-r): Men-Thy-Tol rub for cold control, Gattis Chemical Co., Nashville, Tennessee; Camthomint, vaporizing ointment; Antiseptic Ointment, Pfeiffer Chemical, New York; Brame's Vapomonia Salve, Brame Drug Co., N. Wilksboro, North Carolina; Noxema Skin Cream; McQueen's Pure Mutton Tallow, M.J. Baker Mfg., Nunelly, Tennessee; Gray's Ointment, W.F. Gray Co., Nashville, Tennessee. Bottom (l-r): Toilet Essence; Di-Er-Kiss (2), Kerkoff, New York; Mavis Talcum, Vivaudou, Paris-New York; Lilacs & Roses Talc, Lander, New York; Foley's Cream, Foley & Co., Chicago; Admiration Shampoo. *Courtesy of John & Elsie Booker, Patterson's Mill Country Store, Chapel Hill.*

Powders and scents. Top (l-r): Albolene Baby Powder, McKesson & Robbins, New York; Dr. Palmer's Almomeal tin, Holton & Adams, New York; Doris Powder jar; Ben Hur Powder jar; Mavis Talcum, New York; Mennen's Toilet Powder; Lee's Princess Toilet Talcum, Lee Mfg., Pittsburgh, Pennsylvania; powder jar. Bottom (l-r): Yardley Talc Powder; Plough's Black & White Talcum; Melba Bouquet perfume bottle; Narcissus Eau de Toilet, Bouton, New York; Hoyt's Genuine Cologne, F. Hoyt & Co., New York (3); Sweet Jasmine Silk Sifted Talc, Lander Perfumer, New York; Cashmere Bouquet Talc Powder. *Courtesy of John & Elsie Booker, Patterson's Mill Country Store, Chapel Hill.*

Perfume bottles (l-r): Vain, Tilford; Blue Fern Cologne; Cucumber Jelly, W.H. Brown, Baltimore; L'Aimant Perfume de Toilette. *Courtesy of John & Elsie Booker, Patterson's Mill Country Store, Chapel Hill.*

Three perfume bottles. The one on the left is unmarked except for a raised "R" in the stopper. The center is Mellier's Melodie and on the right is Black Tulip Philonel, Henry Tetlow, Philadelphia. *Courtesy of John & Elsie Booker, Patterson's Mill Country Store, Chapel Hill.*

Four perfumes from the Mellier Co., New York: Belle's Lilac, Sweet Pea, Jockey Club, and Perfume Ideal.

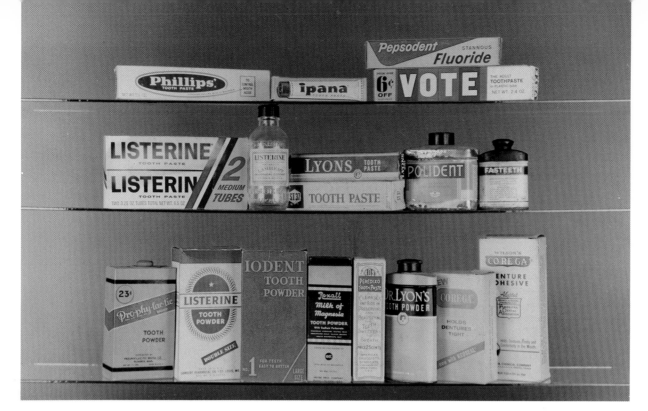

Tooth and mouth care. Top (l-r): Phillip's Tooth Paste, the Chas. H. Phillips Co., Sterling Drugs, New York; Ipana tooth paste, Bristol-Myers, New York; Pepsodent tooth paste, Laver Brothers, New York; Vote tooth paste, Bristol Myers, New York, 1966. Middle (l-r): Listerine tooth paste and mouth wash, Warner-Lambert, Morris Plains, New Jersey; Lyons tooth paste, R.L. Watkins, Sterling Drugs; S.T. 37 toothpaste, Caprokol; Polident tin; Fasteeth tin.

Bottom (l-r): Pro-phy-lac-tic Tooth Powder, Pro-phy-lac-tic Brush Co., Florence, Massachusetts; Listerine Tooth Powder, Lambert Pharmaceutical, St. Louis; Iodent Tooth Powder; Rexall Milk of Magnesia, United Drug Co., Boston; Peredixo Tooth Paste, American Druggist's Syndicate, New York; Dr. Lyon's Tooth Powder, Wilson's Co-Re-Ga Denture Adhesive (2). *Courtesy of John & Elsie Booker, Patterson's Mill Country Store, Chapel Hill.*

Dental care items from the 1920s. Left-right: Septikol Dental Cream; Mineral Tooth Powder, Bloomingdale, Michigan; Listerine toothbrush and porcelain brush sterilizer; Bertram's Tooth Cavity Seal, Dean's

Laboratories, Chicago; Dr. E.A. Welter's Wonderful Tooth Powder; Drucker's Revelation Tooth Powder; Dr. E.L. Graves Unequaled Tooth Powder. *Courtesy of Hook's Historic Drug Store & Pharmacy Museum, Indianapolis.*

Left-right: Pro-phy-lac-tic toothbrushes, sample tin of Wilson's Co-Re-Ga Powdered denture adhesive; Dr. Bonker's Tooth Powder, Dr. Bonker's Medicine Co., Chicago; Drucker's Revelation Tooth Powder box, August E. Drucker Co., San Francisco; Smoker's Nico-Stain Tooth Cleanser tin; Dr. E.A. Welter's Wonderful Tooth Powder tin; Doctor Ellis' F-E-I Tooth Paste, Pyorrhea Specific; The Preventol Laboratories, Pittsburgh. *Courtesy of Hook's Historic Drug Store & Pharmacy Museum, Indianapolis.*

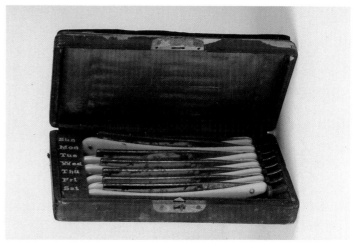

Anchor Brand Seven-day Straight Edge set, Webster Bros., Germany. Ivory handles and steel blades with a leather case, 1.5" x 7" x 4". *Courtesy of Hook's Historic Drug Store & Pharmacy Museum, Indianapolis.*

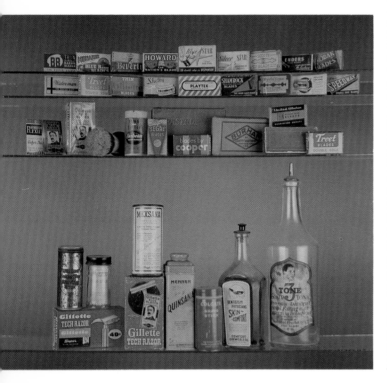

Shaving needs. Top (l-r): BB razor blades, Butler Bros., Chicago; Monaker Blue Razor Blades; Beverly; Howard blades; Blue Star blades; Silver Star, American Safety Razor Corp., Brooklyn; Scotty blades; Enders, Mystic, Connecticut; Probak Blades, Gillette. Second shelf (l-r): Waterman, the Perfect Blade; Treet, Treet Safety Razor Corp., Brooklyn; Gillette, Boston, Massachusetts; Shelby blades; Playtex blades; Shamrock blades, distributed by American News Co., Inc., New York; Goldtone, Goldtone Razor Blade Co., Newark, New Jersey. Pal Hollowground, New York; Speedway, Int'l Safety Razor Co., Bloomfield, New Jersey. Third row (l-r): Feather Edge Flexible; Gillette Blue Blades (2 sizes), Boston; shaving brush; packaging for an attachment to the Sunbeam Shavemaster electric razor; Segal blades; Fastrop sharpener, Chicago; Cooper blades, Cooper Razor Blade Co., Brooklyn, New York; Burham Safety Razor Co. box, New York; United Whelan blades, Whelan Store Corp., New York; Stanford blades; Treet blades, Brooklyn. Bottom (l-r): William's Holder Top Shaving Stick, tin; Gillette Tech razor (2), Gillette, Boston; Mexsana Mexican Heat Powder, Plough Co.; Mennen Quinsana, The Mennen Co., Newark, New Jersey; Colgate Shave Stick; Dentist's and Physician's Skin Comfort, Comfort Chemical, Randallstown, Maryland; Three Tone Scalp Tonic, Eau Claire, Wisconsin. *Courtesy of John & Elsie Booker, Patterson's Mill Country Store, Chapel Hill.*

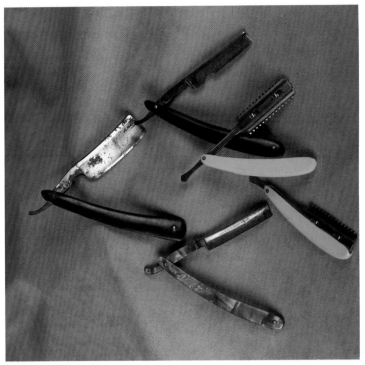

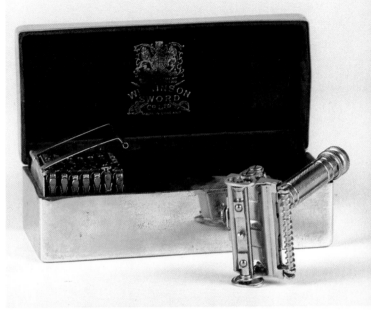

Five straight edge razors. *Courtesy of Hook's Historic Drug Store & Pharmacy Museum, Indianapolis.*

Wilkinson Sword seven day razor set with one handle and seven blades. Stainless steel box lined with velvet, 2.5" x 5" x 1.5". *Courtesy of Hook's Historic Drug Store & Pharmacy Museum, Indianapolis.*

Five razor sets. Left to right: Gillette "Aristocrat"; Gillette; Gillette Khaki Set in a Khaki cover case; Valet Auto-Strop Razor; Ever-Ready Shaving kit. *Courtesy of Hook's Historic Drug Store & Pharmacy Museum, Indianapolis.*

Sharpening devices. Left: Twinplex Stropper, Twinplex Sales Co., St. Louis, Missouri, 3" x 2.5", stainless steel. Center: Fastrop Razorblade Sharpener, the Fastrop Co., Chicago, Illinois. 1" x 2.5" x 1.5". Right: Carborundum sharpening stone, Carborundum Co., Niagara Falls, New York. 2.25" x 6.25" x 0.5". *Courtesy of Hook's Historic Drug Store & Pharmacy Museum, Indianapolis.*

Vibro-Shave Electric Razor, Electric Razor Corporation, New York. This ran on 110 volts and is similar to concept to a razor reintroduced in the late 1980s. Original cost: $5. *Courtesy of Hook's Historic Drug Store & Pharmacy Museum, Indianapolis.*

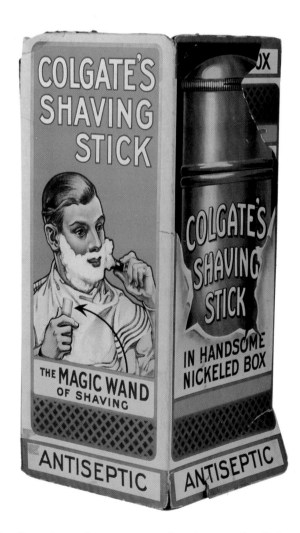

Cardboard stand-up counter advertisement for Colgate's Shaving Stick, 17" x 7.5" x 7.5". *Courtesy of Hook's Historic Drug Store & Pharmacy Museum, Indianapolis.*

Valet AutoStrop Razor advertisement. Paper, 15" x 10". *Courtesy of Hook's Historic Drug Store & Pharmacy Museum, Indianapolis.*

Koin Pack Prophylactics, L.E. Shunk, Akron. The box reads: "Koin Pack Prophylactics are sold only for the prevention of disease-Three gold coins to a package. This box is 2" x 7.5" x 5.5". *Courtesy of John & Elsie Booker, Patterson's Mill Country Store, Chapel Hill.*

Soaps and hair care products. Top (l-r): Bermarine Sta-So Hair Tone Up, Atlanta, Georgia; Bermarine Shampoo and Skin Soap;; Woodbury Facial Soap; Lifebuoy Health Soap; Camay, Poslam Soap, Emergency Laboratories, Jersey City, New Jersey. Middle (l-r): Palmer's Skin Success Ointment box and Hair Success tin, Morgan Drug Co., New York, Kotalko scalp treatment, Kotalko Sales Company, Jersey City, New Jersey; Medalo pressing compound for glamorous hair, Gold Medal Hair Products, New York; Queen Hair Dressing tins (2), Newbro Manufacturing, Atlanta, Georgia; Henna San for the Hair, Lehn & Fink, Bloomfield, New Jersey; B. Paul's Compound for Gray Hair tin, Paul's, New York; Druggists Henna Powder, Penslar Company, New York. Bottom (l-r): Parker's Hair Balsam; White's Specific Face Cream, White's Specific Company, Nashville, Tennessee; Keepya Hair Tonic; Eau Sublime hair coloring, The Guilmard Co., Coral Gables, Florida; Herpicide for Scalp and Hair, The Herpicide Company, New York; Kolor-bak hair color; Mary T. Goldman's Gray Hair Coloring Preparation, Mary T. Goldman Co., St. Paul, Minnesota. *Courtesy of John & Elsie Booker, Patterson's Mill Country Store, Chapel Hill.*

Skin and hair care products. Top (l-r): Bermarine Vanishing Creme; Washington Belle Hair Victory tin; Stacomb; Mogro hair straightener, Black & White Products, Plough Inc., New York; Tip Top Hair Dressing tin, Dawson Mfg. Co., Apex Scalp Cream. Middle (l-r): Usola Hair Tonic; Lucky Tiger Hair Dressing, Lucky Tiger Manufacturing Co, Kansas City, Missouri; Color shampoo; Canthrox Hair Shampoo, H.A. Peterson Co., Chicago; Hair Fix hair dressing; Glo-Co Hair Dressing; Vaseline Hair Tonic, Cheesebrough Mfg. Co., New York. Bottom (l-r): Pamper Shampoo by Toni; Jeris Hair Oil for Dry Scalp; Hirsutone, Nyal Company, Detroit; OJ's Beauty Lotion, Nylotis Quinine and Sage Hair Tonic, Nyal Company, Detroit; Jeris Hair Tonic; Swift Dandruff Treatment; DeWitt's Saponified Cocoanut Oil Shampoo, E.C. DeWitt & Co., Chicago. *Courtesy of John & Elsie Booker, Patterson's Mill Country Store, Chapel Hill.*

Swift Antiseptic Hair Tonic and Shampoo Mix, T.W. Swift Company, Winston-Salem, North Carolina. *Courtesy of John & Elsie Booker, Patterson's Mill Country Store, Chapel Hill.*

Madam C.J. Walker's Wonderful Hair Grower, Madam C.J. Walker Manufacturing Co., Indianapolis, Indiana. C.J. Walker was an early black entrepreneur who developed a line of hair care products for African-Americans. Tin, 2.75″ x .75″. *Courtesy of Hook's Historic Drug Store & Pharmacy Museum, Indianapolis.*

"Boye" Brand needles and shuttles dispenser, c. 1910, The Boye Needle Co., Chicago. The after turning the pointer to the style desired, the shopper opens the sliding door and chooses the needle she wants. Tin, 16″ in diameter x 3.75″ deep. *Courtesy of Hook's Historic Drug Store & Pharmacy Museum, Indianapolis.*

Bottles from hair care products. Left: Tono-Scalpa for Dandruff; right: Colgate & Co., New York. *Courtesy of John & Elsie Booker, Patterson's Mill Country Store, Chapel Hill.*

While not exactly personal care in the pharmaceutical understanding of the word, old drugstores and new had general merchandise that was needed in the home. This ribbon cabinet is at the Hoop's pharmacy museum. It was made by A.N. Russell & Sons, Ilion, New York. Oak and glass, 26″ x 27″ x 7″. *Courtesy of Hook's Historic Drug Store & Pharmacy Museum, Indianapolis.*

A variety of baby bottles. *Courtesy of Hook's Historic Drug Store & Pharmacy Museum, Indianapolis.*

Assorted products (l-r): ear syringe; rectal syringe; glass and rubber breast pump; nipple, graduated bottle with nipple; Davel rubber breast shield, glass and rubber breast shield; bottle caps, antique baby bottle. *Courtesy of John & Elsie Booker, Patterson's Mill Country Store, Chapel Hill.*

Left-right: E-Z baby bottle with embossed baby; graduated baby bottle; baby bottle with India rubber nipple; two early baby bottles, glass breast shield with rubber nipple. *Courtesy of Hook's Historic Drug Store & Pharmacy Museum, Indianapolis.*

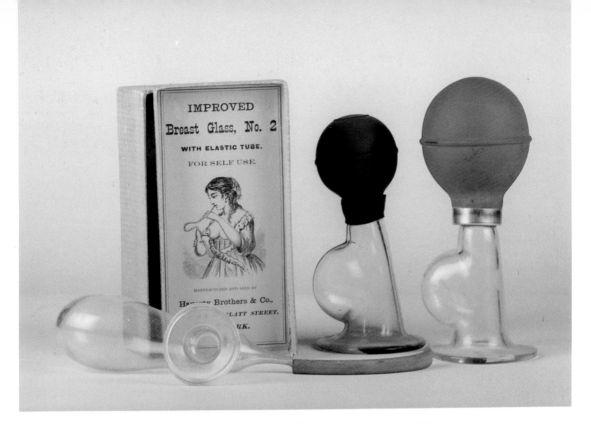

Left: Hagerty Bros., Breast Glass No. 2, operated by sucking on the rubber tube until milk was expressed. Middle: an early breast pump with India rubber bulb. Right: later breast pump.

Nursing bottles. Front row (l-r): Baby's Delighted, nicely decorated bottle; graduated bottle; bottle heavily decorated with the form of a baby; The Original Nurser. Back row (l-r): A & M Co., Universal Feeder; Acme Nursing Bottle, TW Co.; The Little Papoose.

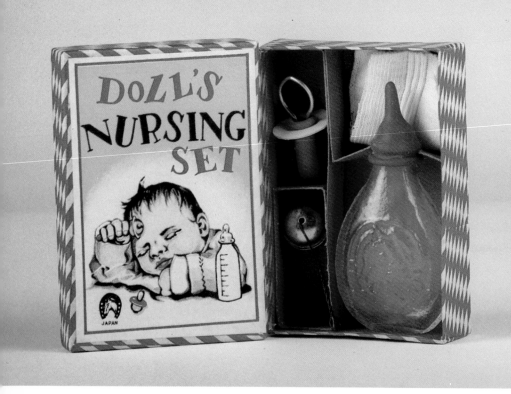

Doll's Nursing Set, Japan. The bottle is glass and is 3″ tall. *Courtesy of Hook's Historic Drug Store & Pharmacy Museum, Indianapolis.*

Large display jar for Faultless Wonder Nipples. The simulated rubber top is actually frosted glass. 13″ x 8.5″. *Courtesy of Hook's Historic Drug Store & Pharmacy Museum, Indianapolis.*

Baby powder tins. Left: Johnson's, Johnson & Johnson, New Brunswick, New Jersey, 3.5″ tall; right, Nelson's Baby Powder, The Penslar Company, Detroit, 5″ tall. *Courtesy of Hook's Historic Drug Store & Pharmacy Museum, Indianapolis.*

144

TOBACCO

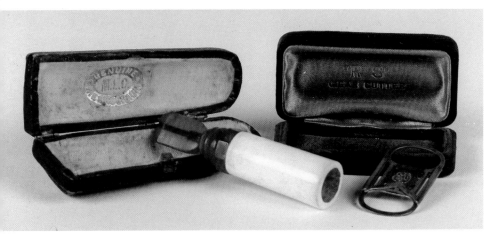

Left: Meerschaum cigar holder in a leather case marked M.L.C. Genuine Meerschaum, c. 1910. 4" long. Right: a personal cigar cutter in its own case, marked "RS Cigar Cutter. 2.25" x 1". *Courtesy of Hook's Historic Drug Store & Pharmacy Museum, Indianapolis.*

Glass Muriel Cigar change tray and a pipe tamper advertising the A. Kefer Drug Co., Indianapolis, High Grade Cigars. *Courtesy of Hook's Historic Drug Store & Pharmacy Museum, Indianapolis.*

Assorted tobacco packages and a pack of LLF papers. *Courtesy of Hook's Historic Drug Store & Pharmacy Museum, Indianapolis.*

A rare Bull Durham Poster, perhaps the only one that includes a cow. Paper, 19.5″ x 13.5″. *Courtesy of John & Elsie Booker, Patterson's Mill Country Store, Chapel Hill.*

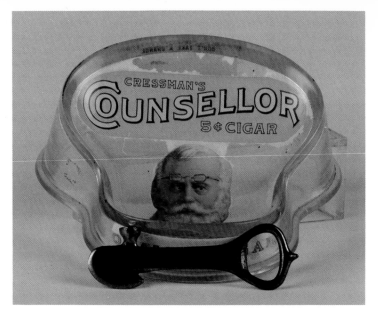

A glass change tray for the counter advertising Cressman's Counsellor 5-cent Cigar, and a combination bottle opener and pipe tamper advertising "Don Antonio Havana Cigars." H. Anton Bock & Co., New York, 4.75″. *Courtesy of Hook's Historic Drug Store & Pharmacy Museum, Indianapolis.*

Left: A decorative brass cigar snip designed to be worn around ones neck on a ribbon. Right: An Anheuser-Busch pocket knife with cork screw, bottle opener, and two blades, dated 1900. Metal, 3.25″. *Courtesy of Hook's Historic Drug Store & Pharmacy Museum, Indianapolis.*

Assorted packaged tobaccos. Left to right: Duke's Mixture, Liggett Myers Tobacco, Durham; F&M Herbs Smoking Tobacco, Hudson, New York; Hiawatha, Spaulding & Merrick, Chicago; Sweet Caporal; Richmond Gem, Allen & Ginter/The American Tobacco Co., Richmond. *Courtesy of Hook's Historic Drug Store & Pharmacy Museum, Indianapolis.*

Counter top cigar cutter, c. 1906. Advertising Havana Cigars, it was made by Brunhoff Manufacturing Co., Cincinnati, Ohio. Cast iron, 8″ x 9″. *Courtesy of Hook's Historic Drug Store & Pharmacy Museum, Indianapolis.*

Countertop cigar cutter and lighter advertising Dean's Old Style Cigar. W.O. Dean Co., Canton, Illinois. Iron, 11.5″ x 6″. *Courtesy of Hook's Historic Drug Store & Pharmacy Museum, Indianapolis.*

Lorillard's Climax Plug tobacco cutter, the Penn Hardware Co., Reading, Pennsylvania. Cast iron, 6″ x 16.5″. *Courtesy of Hook's Historic Drug Store & Pharmacy Museum, Indianapolis.*

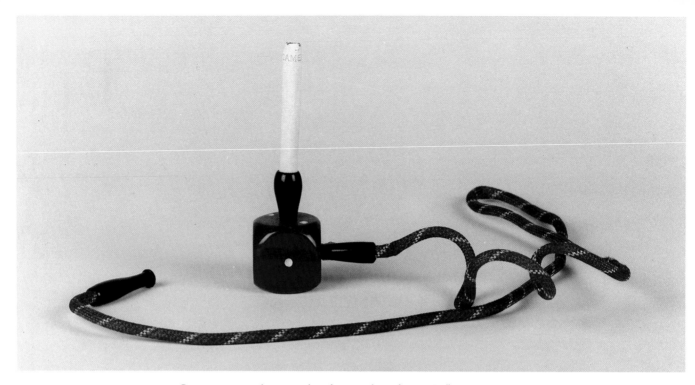

Cigarette smoker in the form of a die. 1.25" square.
*Courtesy of Hook's Historic Drug Store & Pharmacy
Museum, Indianapolis.*

El Gallo tin plate, dated 1905. Vienna Art Plates, 10" in
diameter. *Courtesy of Hook's Historic Drug Store &
Pharmacy Museum, Indianapolis.*

Zig-Zag Cigarette Papers tin display dispenser. 6" x 3.5" x
2". *Courtesy of Hook's Historic Drug Store & Pharmacy
Museum, Indianapolis.*

One pound snuff ball, c. 1910. American Snuff Co., Memphis, originated by Levi Garrett & Sons, Philadelphia. *Courtesy of Hook's Historic Drug Store & Pharmacy Museum, Indianapolis.*

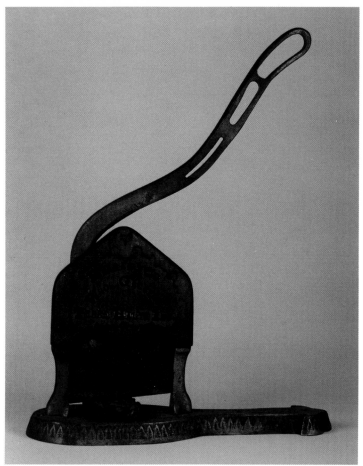

Countertop plug cutter, Hulman & Co., Wholesale Grocers, Terre Haute, Indiana. 9″ x 3″. *Courtesy of Hook's Historic Drug Store & Pharmacy Museum, Indianapolis.*

The Midland Jump Spark Cigar Lighter, c. 1910-1920. Davenport Manufacturing Company, Davenport, Iowa. *Courtesy of Hook's Historic Drug Store & Pharmacy Museum, Indianapolis.*

93 Cigar Cuttings from John Weisert Tobacco Co., St. Louis, Missouri. Paper, 5″ x 3.5″ x 1.75″. *Courtesy of Hook's Historic Drug Store & Pharmacy Museum, Indianapolis.*

Humidor stones like this one were soaked in water and placed in the tobacco display case where the evaporating water kept the tobacco fresh. 7.5″ x 3.5″. *Courtesy of Hook's Historic Drug Store & Pharmacy Museum, Indianapolis.*

La Palina Cigar display jar. Glass, 7″ x 6″. *Courtesy of Hook's Historic Drug Store & Pharmacy Museum, Indianapolis.*

Diamond Matches dispenser. Tin, 13″ x 6″ x 3.5″. *Courtesy of John & Elsie Booker, Patterson's Mill Country Store, Chapel Hill.*

CANDY, GUN AND STAMPS: DISPLAY JARS AND COIN-OPS

Glass display jar with a silverplated lid. The lid is marked Empire Silver Co., Sheffield, England. 9" x 6". *Courtesy of Hook's Historic Drug Store & Pharmacy Museum, Indianapolis.*

A Rexall Drug glass display jar, 4.5" x 5". *Courtesy of Koehler Bros. Inc.—The General Store, Lafayette, Indiana.*

Nut jar from the American Nut Company. Glass, 12″ x 10″. *Courtesy of Hook's Historic Drug Store & Pharmacy Museum, Indianapolis.*

Etched glass jar for Adam's Pure Chewing Gum. 11″ x 5″. *Courtesy of Hook's Historic Drug Store & Pharmacy Museum, Indianapolis.*

Planter's Peanut jar. Glass, 12″ x 8.5″. *Courtesy of Hook's Historic Drug Store & Pharmacy Museum, Indianapolis.*

Counter display jar, probably for candy. Glass, 9″ x 4″.
*Courtesy of Hook's Historic Drug Store & Pharmacy
Museum, Indianapolis.*

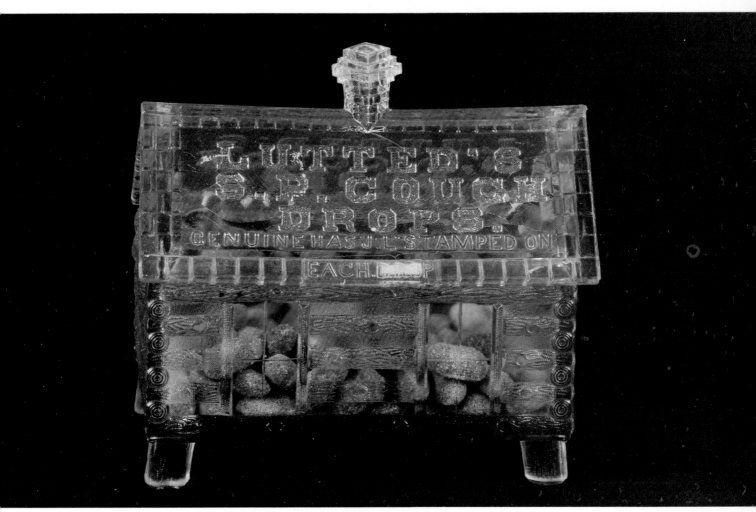

Cabin-shaped glass container for Liltted's S.P. Cough
Drops. 7″ x 7.75″ x 5″. *Courtesy of Hook's Historic Drug
Store & Pharmacy Museum, Indianapolis.*

Tin Yucatan Gum counter display. The American Chicle Co., c. 1900. 6″ x 7″ x 5″. *Courtesy of Hook's Historic Drug Store & Pharmacy Museum, Indianapolis.*

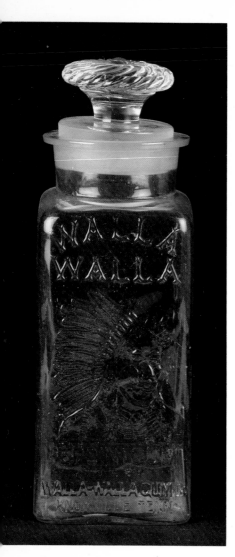

Counter display jar for Walla Walla Pepsin Gum, Walla Walla Gum Co., Knoxville, Tennessee. Glass, 13.5″ x 5″. *Courtesy of Hook's Historic Drug Store & Pharmacy Museum, Indianapolis.*

Coin operated Zeno Chewing Gum dispenser, c. 1900-1920. Tin and wood, 16″ x 10″ x 7.5″. Loaned by the Wm. Wrigley Co. *Courtesy of Hook's Historic Drug Store & Pharmacy Museum, Indianapolis.*

This ball gum machine had the added incentive of the slot machine. While a penny's worth of gum was guaranteed, you were also entitled to a pull of the lever, though it is unclear if you won any thing for a match. The symbols on the wheel were popular cigarette brands of the day. Chewing gum was often marketed as a way of taking away the effects of tobacco on the breath and taste buds. Cast iron and wood, 11.5" x 10.5" x 7.5". *Courtesy of Hook's Historic Drug Store & Pharmacy Museum, Indianapolis.*

This coin operated gum machine had the added incentive of winning free gum. When you put a penny in the wheel spun. While a penny's worth was guaranteed, if the wheel stopped at the right spot you would get an extra piece of gum. Wm. Wrigley Jr. & Co., c. 1900. Loaned by the Wm. Wrigley Co. *Courtesy of Hook's Historic Drug Store & Pharmacy Museum, Indianapolis.*

Inside of above ball gum machine.

Peanut vending machine of cast iron, tin, and glass, with a porcelain cup. Brice Williams Co., Kokomo, Indiana. 19″ x 8″ x 8″. *Courtesy of Hook's Historic Drug Store & Pharmacy Museum, Indianapolis.*

Stainless steel pack gum counter dispenser. 14″ x 8″. *Courtesy of Hook's Historic Drug Store & Pharmacy Museum, Indianapolis.*

Metal and glass ball gum Machine, c. 1910, Advance Machine Company, Chicago. 13" tall. *Courtesy of Hook's Historic Drug Store & Pharmacy Museum, Indianapolis.*

Ball gum machine. Iron and glass, 16.5" x 7". *Courtesy of Hook's Historic Drug Store & Pharmacy Museum, Indianapolis.*

Ball gum machine by the Columbus Vending Co., Columbus, Ohio. 16.5" tall. *Courtesy of Hook's Historic Drug Store & Pharmacy Museum, Indianapolis.*

Cast iron ball gum and fortune machine, coin operated.
Cast iron, 8″ x 13″ x 9.5″. *Courtesy of Hook's Historic Drug
Store & Pharmacy Museum, Indianapolis.*

Aspirin was also available in vending machines. For a nickel
you would get four Blackhawk Brand aspirin tablets of five
grains each. Blackhawk Specialty Co., Silvis, Illinois. Cast
iron and wood, 12″ x 6.5″ x 5.5″. *Courtesy of Hook's
Historic Drug Store & Pharmacy Museum, Indianapolis.*

Coin operated dispenser for Wilbur-Suchard Chocolates.
O.J. Miles, Exclusive Distributor, Chicago, c. 1900.
*Courtesy of Hook's Historic Drug Store & Pharmacy
Museum, Indianapolis.*

Cast iron postage stamp machine. 14″ x 12.5″ x 8″. *Courtesy of Hook's Historic Drug Store & Pharmacy Museum, Indianapolis.*

World War I era postage stamp machine, Schermack Products Corporation, Detroit. Metal and glass, 13″ x 7″ x 7″. *Courtesy of Hook's Historic Drug Store & Pharmacy Museum, Indianapolis.*

The corner drugstore was also a convenient place to get stamps. Nearly every store had a stamp machine. This Kone Klutch machine, of wood, steel, and glass, with a tin sign, had a scale on the top for weighing one's letter. Federal Stamp Machine Co., Minneapolis, Minnesota. 11″ x 13″ x 10″. *Courtesy of Hook's Historic Drug Store & Pharmacy Museum, Indianapolis.*

Bibliography

Armour, Richard. *Drug Store Days: My Youth Among the Pills and Potions.* New York: MacGraw-HIll Book Company, Inc., 1959.

Bergevin, Al. *Drugstore Tins & Their Prices.* Radnor, Pennsylvania: Wallace-Homestead Book Company, 1990.

Carson, Gerald. *One for a Man, Two for a Horse: A Pictorial History, Grave & Comic, of Patent Medicines.* Garden City, New York: Doubleday & Company, Inc., 1961.

Congdon-Martin, Douglas, with Robert Biondi. *Country Store Collectibles.* West Chester, Pennsylvania: Schiffer Publishing, 1990.

Congdon-Martin, Douglas. *America for Sale: A Collector's Guide to Antique Advertising.* West Chester, Pennsylvania: Schiffer Publishing, 1990.

Foster, Lawrence G. *A Company that Cares: One Hundred Year Illustrated History of Johnson & Johnson.* New Brunswick, New Jersey: Johnson & Johnson, 1986.

Hechtlinger, Adelaide. *The Great Patent Medicine Era, or Without Benefit of Doctor.* New York: Galahad Books, 1970.

Official Guide to Bottles Old and New, The, (tenth edition). New York: House of Collectibles, 1986

Sellari, Carlo & Dorothy. *The Standard Old Bottle Price Guide.* Paducah, Kentucky: Collector Books, 1989.

Young, James Harvey. *The Toadstool Millionaires: A Social History of Patent Medicines in America before Federal Regulations.* Princeton: Princeton University Press, 1972.

Footnotes

[1] Richard Armour, *Drug Store Days: My LIfe Among the Pills and Potions,* (New York: McGraw-Hill Book Company, Inc., 1959), p. 62

[1] *Ibid.,* p. 57

[3] *Ibid.,* p. 59

[4] James Harvey Young, *The Toadstool Millionaires: A Social History of Patent Medicines in America before Federal Regulations,* (Princeton: Princeton University Press, 1972), p. 7.

[5] *Ibid.,* p. 10.

[6] *Ibid.,* p. 14.

[7] *Ibid.,* p. 40ff.

[8] *Ibid.,* p. 37

[9] Gerald Carson, *One for a Man, Two for a Horse: A Pictorial History, Grave & Comic, of Patent Medicines,* (Garden City, New York: Doubleday & Company, Inc., 1961), p. 8ff.

[10] Armour, *Op. cit.,* p. 60.